REVELATION

BOOKS OF FAITH SERIES
Leader Session Guide

Eric D. Barreto

AUGSBURG FORTRESS
Minneapolis

REVELATION
Leader Session Guide

Books of Faith Series
Book of Faith Adult Bible Studies

Copyright © 2012 Augsburg Fortress. All rights reserved. Except for brief quotations in critical articles or reviews, no part of this book may be reproduced in any manner without prior written permission from the publisher. For more information, visit: www.augsburgfortress.org/copyrights or write to: Permissions, Augsburg Fortress, Box 1209, Minneapolis, MN 55440-1209.

Book of Faith is an initiative of the
Evangelical Lutheran Church in America
 God's work. Our hands.

For more information about the Book of Faith initiative, go to www.bookoffaith.org.

Scripture quotations, unless otherwise marked, are from New Revised Standard Version Bible, copyright © 1989 Division of Christian Education of the National Council of Churches of Christ in the United States of America. Used by permission. All rights reserved.

References to ELW are from *Evangelical Lutheran Worship* (Augsburg Fortress, 2006).

Photos on page 24 by Eric D. Barreto. Used by permission.

Web site addresses are provided in this resource for your use. These listings do not represent an endorsement of the sites by Augsburg Fortress, nor do we vouch for their content for the life of this resource.

ISBN: 978-1-4514-0277-3
Writer: Eric D. Barreto
Cover and interior design: Spunk Design Machine, spkdm.com
Typesetting: PerfecType, Nashville, TN

The paper used in this publication meets the minimum requirements of American National Standard for Information Sciences—Permanence of Paper for Printed Library Materials, ANSI Z329.48-1984.

Manufactured in the U.S.A.
18 17 16 15 14 13 12 1 2 3 4 5 6 7 8 9 10

CONTENTS

	Introduction	5
1	**Revealing Revelation** *Revelation 1:1-20*	9
2	**Life and Faith in Pergamum and Laodicea** *Revelation 2:12-17; 3:14-22*	19
3	**Visions of God and the Lamb** *Revelation 4:1-6a; 5:1-10*	29
4	**Destruction and Protection** *Revelation 6:15—7:17*	38
5	**The Great "Battle"** *Revelation 12:1-17*	47
6	**The Fall of a Great and Powerful Empire** *Revelation 18:1-24*	56
7	**Our New Home Is Here but Not Here** *Revelation 21:1-8*	64
8	**Jesus Is Coming Soon** *Revelation 22:8-21*	73

Introduction

Book of Faith Adult Bible Studies

Welcome to the conversation! The Bible study resources you are using are created to support the bold vision of the Book of Faith initiative that calls "the whole church to become more fluent in the first language of faith, the language of Scripture, in order that we might live into our calling as a people renewed, enlivened, empowered, and sent by the Word."

Simply put, this initiative and these resources invite you to "Open Scripture. Join the Conversation."

We enter into this conversation based on the promise that exploring the Bible deeply with others opens us to God working in and through us. God's Word is life changing, church changing, and world changing. Lutheran approaches to Scripture provide a fruitful foundation for connecting Bible, life, and faith.

A Session Overview

Each session is divided into the following four key sections. The amount of time spent in each section may vary based on choices you make. The core Learner Session Guide is designed for 50 minutes. A session can be expanded to as much as 90 minutes by using the Bonus Activities that appear in the Leader Session Guide.

- **Gather (10-15 minutes)**
Time to check in, make introductions, review homework assignments, share an opening prayer, and use the Focus Activity to introduce learners to the Session Focus.

- **Open Scripture (10-15 minutes)**
The session Scripture text is read using a variety of methods and activities. Learners are asked to respond to a few general questions. As leader, you may want to capture initial thoughts or questions on paper for later review.

- **Join the Conversation (25-55 minutes)**
Learners explore the session Scripture text through core questions and activities that cover each of the four perspectives (see diagram on p. 6). The core Learner Session Guide material may be expanded through use of the Bonus Activities provided in the Leader Session Guide. Each session ends with a brief Wrap-up and prayer.

- **Extending the Conversation (5 minutes)**
Lists homework assignments, including next week's session Scripture text. The leader may choose one or more items to assign for all. Each session also includes additional Enrichment options and may include For Further Reading suggestions.

A Method to Guide the Conversation

Book of Faith Adult Bible Studies has three primary goals:

- To increase biblical fluency;
- To encourage and facilitate informed small group conversation based on God's Word; and
- To renew and empower us to carry out God's mission for the sake of the world.

To accomplish these goals, each session will explore one or more primary Bible texts from four different angles and contexts—historical, literary, Lutheran, and devotional. These particular ways of exploring a text are not new, but used in combination they provide a full understanding of and experience with the text.

Complementing this approach is a commitment to engaging participants in active, learner-orientated Bible conversations. The resources call for prepared leaders to facilitate learner discovery, discussion, and activity. Active learning and frequent engagement with Scripture will lead to greater biblical fluency and encourage active faith.

1 We begin by reading the Bible text and reflecting on its meaning. We ask questions and identify items that are unclear. We bring our unique background and experience to the Bible, and the Bible meets us where we are.

5 We return to where we started, but now we have explored and experienced the Bible text from four different dimensions. We are ready to move into the "for" dimension. We have opened Scripture and joined in conversation for a purpose. We consider the meaning of the text for faithful living. We wonder what God is calling us (individually and as communities of faith) to do. We consider how God's Word is calling us to do God's work in the world.

2* We seek to understand the world of the Bible and locate the setting of the text. We explore who may have written the text and why. We seek to understand the particular social and cultural contexts that influenced the content and the message. We wonder who the original audience may have been. We think about how these things "translate" to our world today.

Devotional Context

Historical Context

Lutheran Context

Literary Context

4 We consider the Lutheran principles that help ground our interpretation of the Bible text. We ask questions that bring those principles and unique Lutheran theological insights into conversation with the text. We discover how our Lutheran insights can ground and focus our understanding and shape our faithful response to the text.

3* We pay close attention to how the text is written. We notice what kind of literature it is and how this type of literature may function or may be used. We look at the characters, the story line, and the themes. We compare and contrast these with our own understanding and experience of life. In this interchange, we discover meaning.

* Sessions may begin with either Historical Context or Literary Context.

The diagram on page 6 summarizes the general way this method is intended to work. A more detailed introduction to the method used in Book of Faith Adult Bible Studies is available in *Opening the Book of Faith* (Augsburg Fortress, 2008).

The Learner Session Guide

The Learner Session Guide content is built on the four sections (see p. 5). The content included in the main "Join the Conversation" section is considered to be the core material needed to explore the session Scripture text. Each session includes a Focus Image that is used as part of an activity or question somewhere within the core session. Other visuals (maps, charts, photographs, and illustrations) may be included to help enhance the learner's experience with the text and its key concepts.

The Leader Session Guide

For easy reference, the Leader Session Guide contains all the content included in the Learner Session Guide and more. The elements that are unique to the Leader Session Guide are the following:

- **Before You Begin**—Helpful tips to use as you prepare to lead the session.
- **Session Overview**—Contains detailed description of key themes and content covered in each of the four contexts (Historical, Literary, Lutheran, Devotional). Core questions and activities in the Learner Session Guide are intended to emerge directly from this Session Overview.
- **Key Definitions**—Key terms or concepts that appear in the Session Overview may be illustrated or defined.
- **Facilitator's Prayer**—To help the leader center on the session theme and leadership task.
- **Bonus Activities**—Optional activities included in each of the four sections of "Join the Conversation" used by the leader to expand the core session.
- **Tips**—A variety of helpful hints, instructions, or background content to aid leadership facilitation.
- **Looking Ahead**—Reminders to the leader about preparation for the upcoming session.

Leader and Learner

In Book of Faith Adult Bible Studies, the leader's primary task is facilitating small group conversation and activity. These conversations are built around structured learning tasks. What is a structured learning task? It is an open question or activity that engages learners with new content and the resources they need to respond. Underlying this structured dialog approach are three primary assumptions about adult learners:

- Adult learners bring with them varied experiences and the capability to do active learning tasks;
- Adult learners learn best when they are invited to be actively involved in learning; and
- Adults are more accountable and engaged when active learning tasks are used.

Simply put, the goal is fluency in the first language of faith, the language of Scripture. How does one become fluent in a new language, proficient in building houses, or skilled at hitting a baseball? By practicing and doing in a hands-on way. Book of Faith Adult Bible Studies provides the kind of hands-on Bible exploration that will produce Bible-fluent learners equipped to do God's work in the world.

Books of Faith Series

Book of Faith Adult Bible Studies includes several series and courses. This Revelation unit is part of the Books of Faith Series, which is designed to explore key themes and texts in the books of the Bible. Each book of the Bible reveals a unique story or message of faith. Many core themes and story lines and characters are shared by several books, but each book in its own right is a book of faith. Exploring these books of faith in depth opens us to the variety and richness of God's written word for us.

Revelation Unit Overview

Many people avoid reading Revelation due to fear or confusion. Some of the imagery is violent and fearsome, as even the very foundations of the world are shaken. Making matters more difficult are the various ways the book is read and interpreted in our culture. Is Revelation a precise road map of the last days? Is it a book that can only be interpreted by certain people with special knowledge? Is it better to just leave it alone?

One thing that should shape how we understand Revelation is the long, ever-present shadow of Roman power. Rome's economic, political, and military might was simply part of daily life for John, the writer of Revelation, and the seven churches he addresses. John argues, however, that the power of Rome is illusory and temporary. True power and justice reside only with God, and God's followers will not be left to suffer without comfort and hope.

The genres of writing also shape our understanding of the book. Revelation begins like an ancient letter, or, actually, seven letters to seven churches. Then John begins to describe a revelatory experience, a profound moment of understanding granted by God through Jesus Christ. We will read both the letters and the visions, and think about how they inform each other.

Certainly our understanding of Revelation is also shaped by its heavily symbolic language. Fortunately, Revelation itself interprets some symbols for us, while other symbols trace back to traditions in the Hebrew Bible. It is important, however, not to dwell so much on the most enigmatic portions of the book that we miss the forest for the trees. This study looks at important symbols and keeps the big picture of Revelation in mind.

The central vision of the book is found in Revelation 4–5, where God is on a throne and Jesus is the Lamb who was slain. This vision should also be central to our understanding of the book. Despite all evidence to the contrary, God rules and rules alone. Jesus is made powerful through weakness. God's character and Jesus' faithfulness persevere.

Ultimately, Revelation is not about providing a road map or predictions for the end of days. Instead, it describes a way for us to relate to God and to one another today. It invites us to trust in God and God's work, to look to Jesus' return with hope for a new world, and to read, study, and listen for God speaking to us through these words today.

Session 1, "Revealing Revelation" (Revelation 1:1-20), introduces the book, writer, genre of literature, and role of the Roman Empire.

Session 2, "Life and Faith in Pergamum and Laodicea" (Revelation 2:12-17; 3:14-22), looks at two of the seven letters to churches, showing some of the challenges faced by the earliest Christians.

Session 3, "Visions of God and the Lamb" (Revelation 4:1-6a; 5:1-10), explores the central image in the book. While the God of Revelation is exalted in the highest heavens, this same God is also profoundly concerned with the plight of God's children.

Session 4, "Destruction and Protection" (Revelation 6:15—7:17), shows the two paths taken by this book. While ordeals, tribulations, and plagues characterize both the present and the future, God's promises are ever faithful.

Session 5, "The Great 'Battle'" (Revelation 12:1-17), demonstrates that the result of the great conflicts between God and the forces of evil is clear: God, God's creation, and God's children are victorious.

Session 6, "The Fall of a Great and Powerful Empire" (Revelation 18:1-24), studies the fall of Babylon, a code name for Rome. In the shadow of the Roman Empire, Revelation undermines the power and permanence of the preeminent political force of the ancient world.

Session 7, "Our New Home Is Here but Not Here" (Revelation 21:1-8), deals with the renewed creation that brings to full fruition God's original hopes for the world.

Session 8, "Jesus Is Coming Soon" (Revelation 22:8-21), looks to the future with hope, anticipation, and expectation.

SESSION ONE

Revelation 1:1-20

Leader Session Guide

Focus Statement
Revelation is a difficult but rich text for contemporary Christians to interpret. Paying attention to its historical context, literary features, and theological imagination results in a contemporary, relevant, meaningful, and powerful reading of this book.

Key Verse
Blessed is the one who reads aloud the words of the prophecy, and blessed are those who hear and who keep what is written in it; for the time is near. *Revelation 1:3*

Focus Image

Armageddon ©iStockphoto.com/ Igor Zhuravlov

Revealing Revelation

Session Preparation

Before You Begin . . .

Revelation is a difficult book to read. With powerful and often disturbing images, John leads us into a world of comfort and hope in the midst of persecution. But there is also fear and trepidation as the very foundations of the world are shaken. Making matters even more difficult are the various ways Christians have read this book. Is Revelation a precise sketch of the last days? Is it a word of relief to early Christians that has no relevance to us? Is it something in-between? Something else entirely? In the end, *how* we read is as important as *what* we read in this book.

Session Instructions

1. Read this Session Guide completely and highlight or underline any portions you wish to emphasize with the group. Note any Bonus Activities you wish to do.

2. If you plan to do any special activities, check to see what materials you'll need, if any.

3. Have extra Bibles on hand in case a member of the group forgets to bring one.

Session Overview

Too often, Christians are tempted to avoid reading Revelation. Its powerful images are not easily interpreted. And yet Revelation is a powerful work of theology still relevant for us today. To begin our exploration, we will focus on the historical and literary background of this book and on how Christians have interpreted this book. Basically, we are asking, "What kind of book is this?" and "How do we read it?"

HISTORICAL CONTEXT

The first word in the Greek text of Revelation tells us a great deal about what kind of book this is. The NRSV translates the word as "revelation." The Greek term behind this translation tells us that the **literary genre** of Revelation is **apocalyptic**. It is a revelation of knowledge so powerful and mysterious that humans can only know it if God and God's intermediaries reveal it to us. Revelation 1:3 is therefore not a claim based in John's confidence in his writing as much as a confession that the contents of Revelation are direct from God.

SESSION ONE

 Literary genre:
Literary genres refer to different kinds of writing. For example, we can read something and usually identify pretty quickly whether we are reading a fairy tale, a newspaper article, or an academic paper. Literary genres provide helpful cultural cues for us. Different genres follow certain rules in their composition. What kind of language is used? What images are common? Genre also points to how a piece of literature communicates or in what sense it speaks truth. Think for example of the different insights that a fairy tale and a newspaper article communicate.

 Apocalyptic:
Apocalyptic is a genre of ancient literature but also a worldview. As a genre, apocalyptic usually contains divine communications that were unknowable prior to the "unveiling." (The Greek term behind "apocalypse" literally means "unveiling.") How do humans get to know this knowledge? In apocalyptic, some intermediary—like an angel—serves as a bridge between God and humans. As a worldview, apocalyptic expects God's powerful intervention in history in order to upend the status quo of injustice and unfairness.

 Eschatology:
Eschatology and apocalyptic are often closely aligned. While apocalyptic is primarily a genre and a worldview that often deal with end times, eschatology is an area of theological reflection dealing with the culmination of life as we know it. Eschatology can deal with the end of individual lives but often deals with the culmination of the world as it now is. Simply and in most cases, eschatology is reflection on the end of time as we know it.

Revelation deals with **eschatology**, that is, with a view toward the end or culmination of the world as we know it. Why would John and his first readers be concerned about the end of time? They were concerned not because they were oriented toward the future, but toward a present marked by oppression and trouble. Eschatology, then, is comfort in the midst of tribulation for a powerless people. Revelation argues that the power of Rome is illusory and temporary. True power and justice reside only with God, and God's followers will not be left to suffer without comfort and hope.

The challenge for us today is to imagine ourselves in such a situation. In general, we as Westerners are generally well-off, powerful, and in control of our lives. For the most part, the status quo works *for* us, not *against* us. This was not the case for the early Christians. Looking ahead to God's upending the world brought greater comfort and hope to them than it probably does to most of us. Help participants reflect on the difference between the ancient world and today. Help them also reflect on how Revelation still speaks to us today.

Literary Context

Revelation exhibits at least two different genres of writing. The book begins like an ancient letter, much like Paul's letters to communities of early believers, but something is rather different here. Quickly, John turns to a description of a revelatory experience, a profound moment of understanding granted by God through Jesus Christ. What we have in the book of Revelation is an apocalypse with an opening that reads like a letter. Generally, Christians tend to focus either on the seven letters to the churches or on the visionary details of the remaining chapters. But Revelation's opening verses suggest that we need to read these two parts of Revelation *together*. How do the letters inform the visions and vice versa? Highlight this important question for participants in this session. We will return to it as the study moves along.

The first few verses of Revelation help set our expectations as readers. This is a book with an indispensable, God-breathed message. Its veracity is rooted not in John's authority but in God's direct revelation. What are the implications of such a claim?

The message of Revelation is so profound, so surprising, so unexpected that John frequently opts for heavily symbolic language. We see an excellent example of Revelation's symbolic language in 1:12-16. What does it mean to portray Jesus with seven stars in his hands? What does it mean to portray Jesus with a sword protruding from his mouth?

Fortunately, we have help in interpreting these symbols. First, Revelation itself will interpret some symbols for us. So, according to Revelation 1:20, the seven stars and lampstands are the seven churches and their respective angels. Second, Revelation's symbols are usually not unique to John. He relies on traditions in the Hebrew Bible to craft his symbols. The notes of a good study Bible will point you in the right direction.

Finally, however, it is important not to dwell excessively on the most enigmatic portions of Revelation. Help participants keep their vision wide. What is the big picture? What are the larger theological questions being posed by Revelation? In the study of Revelation, it is best not to miss the forest for the trees.

Lutheran Context

Martin Luther did not hold back in his comments about Revelation. In his 1522 preface to his translation of the book, he expresses doubts over Revelation's place in the canon of Scripture, though he acknowledges his concerns may be largely personal and perhaps not binding on others.

Initially, Luther is concerned that Revelation's consistent use of mysterious images, symbols, and visions does not fit in with the otherwise clear witness of the rest of the Bible. Others, Luther argues, use "clear and plain words" and "I can in no way detect the Holy Spirit produced it." Second, he chides John for valuing his work too highly (see 22:18-19), especially when his writing is so unclear. Furthermore, he notes that a number of the earliest leaders of the church "rejected this book a long time ago." Last, he returns to his personal convictions: "My spirit cannot accommodate itself to this book. . . . Therefore I stick to the books which present Christ to me clearly and purely." (Preface to the Revelation of St. John, 1522, *Luther's Works*, ed. E. Theodore Bachmann [Fortress Press, 1960], pp. 35:399).

Anyone who has spent time with Revelation is likely to relate to Luther's critique. The writer often trades on opaque images. Many have abused these complexities with wild interpretations that seek to draw a one-to-one correlation between the biblical text and specific contemporary events.

Eventually, however, Luther's views on Revelation shifted. Craig Koester observes that "Revelation warns readers not to

SESSION ONE

be deceived into despair. . . . As a promise, Revelation assures readers that if 'the word of the gospel remains pure among us, and we love and cherish it, we shall not doubt that Christ is with us, even when things are at their worst.' For 'through and beyond all plagues, beasts, and evil angels, Christ is nonetheless with his saints and wins the final victory'" (*Revelation and the End of All Things* [Grand Rapids, MI: Eerdmans, 2001], p. 12).

Devotional Context

Why does John appeal to images, symbols, and vision instead of plain language? To be sure, apocalyptic literature tends to draw on such imagery, much like our modern fairy tales appeal to witches and trolls, and histories draw on dates and statistics. But something else might be happening.

John speaks in powerful but enigmatic visions because the message he has received from God through Jesus is itself powerful but enigmatic. Hope in the midst of persecution is difficult to comprehend. Expectation and trust in God's promises are difficult to maintain when the rest of the world seems entirely opposed to you.

Think about a time when you experienced a difficult trial in life. How could you best describe that moment to another person? Would you rather describe it like a journalist or a poet?

Facilitator's Prayer

God of all creation, for your wondrous world, I give you thanks. God of consolation, for the many ways you have brought your grace into my life, I give you thanks. God of all time and space, for walking with me in the past, present, and future, I give you thanks. Open now my mind to read your word and to follow your Spirit where you may lead me. Amen.

Gather (10–15 minutes)

Check-in

Take time to greet each person and invite learners to introduce themselves to one another.

Pray

God of our past, our present, and our future, dwell with us as we open your word. Help us see hope in the midst of despair, expectation in the midst of disappointment, your future in the midst of our present.

Tip:
How well do the participants in this study know each other? Consider ways to introduce or reintroduce the participants to one another. Provide space for participants to share both their names and their stories as they introduce themselves. Even if participants know each other by name, they may not know each other's stories of faith.

SESSION ONE

Grant us eyes to see and ears to hear your word afresh and anew. Amen.

Focus Activity

When someone mentions the end of days or the book of Revelation, what images and thoughts come to mind for you? Write your answer (just a word or two), large enough for others in the group to read it. When you are done, hold up your paper and read what others have written.

Open Scripture (10–15 minutes)

Ask one or several members of the group to read the text. As they read, ask two or three other people to draw what they hear on a whiteboard or several large pieces of chart paper. At the end of the reading, allow time for the artists to explain their work.

Ask one person to read the text while other group members keep a tally of every time a word or a phrase comes up that they don't understand or want to know more about. At the end of the reading, ask a few people to share some of the questions they now have after hearing the text.

Read Revelation 1:1-20.
- What images or words stood out to you during the reading?
- Describe your reactions to this text.
- What questions do you have as you listen to this text?

Join the Conversation (25–55 minutes)

Historical Context

1. We begin our study of Revelation by asking some basic questions. Who wrote this book and why? John identifies himself as the author (1:4). However, it is difficult to pinpoint precisely *which* John actually wrote the text. Was it the John who was one of Jesus' twelve disciples? Was it the individual who wrote the Gospel of John or the letters of John? Reaching a conclusion on these matters is difficult. At the same time, we can learn quite a bit about the relationship between John and those to whom he is writing.

Tip:
Consider using videos from enterthebible.org, a Luther Seminary Web site, as introductions to these sessions. This site includes several short but significant reflections on Revelation and other Scripture texts.

Tip:
Make sure you let participants know they will be sharing their reflections with the rest of the group. While honesty and openness about our encounters with Revelation are the aim, we also want to assure that no one's doubts or questions are aired without their permission.

Tip:
Reading Scripture together is both incredibly rewarding and difficult for many of us, and this is particularly true when we engage with Revelation. As you check in and introduce this study, make it clear that all participants are learners in the process. We all have important, profound questions to bring to the table. Find ways to encourage everyone to participate in discussion. Set the tone as the study leader by sharing the questions, doubts, and excitement you bring to this text.

Tip:
A term like "apocalyptic" or "eschatology" is not part of everyday language for most people. These terms are good shorthand for the study but can also confuse participants who may be hearing or discussing this terminology for the first time. Take the time to make sure everyone has a good grasp of these terms before moving forward. Think of contemporary examples to help illustrate these complicated notions.

- Reread Revelation 1:9-11. It is likely that John finds himself exiled on the island of Patmos by the Roman authorities on account of his faith. What else do we learn about John here?

2. The power of the Roman Empire is always in the background of Revelation. Though the center of power in Rome was geographically distant, the empire's reach was extensive, especially in the region of Asia Minor (modern-day Turkey), where the seven churches addressed by John were located. The island of Patmos is a small island in the Aegean Sea.

- Use the map below to locate the Aegean Sea and to note how much territory was under Roman control.

3. Revelation is a subtly subversive text, trying to make sense of persecution and the oppressiveness of Roman rule by challenging the supremacy of the greatest political power the world had ever seen. One way to challenge Rome's supremacy was by writing an *apocalypse*, a kind of literature present both today and in antiquity. Apocalypses usually deal with end times, but they are even more than that. Apocalyptic is also a way of seeing the world when the world doesn't seem to make any sense. Apocalyptic literature reveals information from God, usually through an angel. This information often sounds strange because it runs contrary to the way the world is currently working. In the case of Revelation, John writes to people—who know full well the broad, almost universal, power of Rome—with a revolutionary idea: Perhaps Rome is not nearly as powerful as it seems. Perhaps Jesus is more powerful than Caesar.

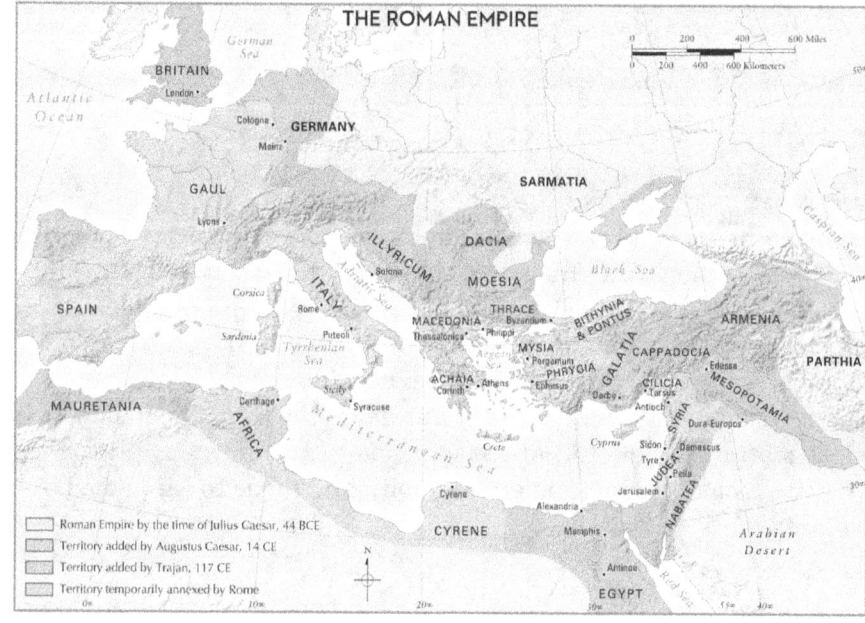

- It is no accident that Jesus is described as "the ruler of the kings of the earth" in Revelation 1:5. Why would this be a revolutionary or even treasonous thing to say in the ancient world?
- Think about what this means for us today. Who or what would be "Rome" now? And are we more like the powerful Romans or the powerless Christians John is hoping to help?

Literary Context

1. Just as the beginning of a book or movie sets the tone for the whole work, the beginning of Revelation sets the tone for the rest of the book.
- Give some examples of movies and books with particularly memorable openings. What makes these so impactful? How do they set up a certain set of expectations about the book you are about to read or the movie you are about to watch?
- Read Revelation 1:1-2 again and identify whose message is in the book and who delivers that message. Why is the source of this message so important to John?
- Now turn to Revelation 1:3. How does John expect his readers and hearers to respond? What does it mean to you that "the time is near"?

2. Revelation often uses symbols and numbers to communicate. (Some are easy to interpret. Others are perplexing.) Figuring out these symbols and numbers is part of our study of this book. Sometimes John reveals their meanings clearly. For example, in Revelation 1:20 Jesus explains that the seven stars he was holding in his right hand represent the angels of the seven churches (which we'll discuss in session 2).
- Read Revelation 1:12-16 again. Make a list of symbols and numbers included in this passage. How can we discern what these might have meant for John and his original readers?
- Make a list of some symbols that are part of our daily lives. How do we know what these mean? Discuss how to determine who is right when a symbol means one thing to one person and something completely different to another.

Bonus Activity:

Revelation is not the only portion of Scripture that trades on apocalyptic language. Read Matthew 24, Mark 13, or Luke 21 and note what Jesus says about "the end." Discuss what it means for our faith that Jesus himself highlighted apocalyptic themes in his ministry.

Bonus Activity:

Turn to Daniel 7, another passage of Scripture that draws upon apocalyptic images and symbols. What similarities can you draw between Daniel 7 and Revelation? Again, we discover here that Revelation is not an innovation in Scripture but part of a larger theological tradition.

Tip:

Another example of the powerful way stories begin is the fairy-tale favorite "Once upon a time." Think for a moment about how much information those four words carry. Those four short words tell you that the genre of the story you are about to hear is a fairy tale. The story will probably involve some elements of fantasy. Finally, the story will end with some moral. From four little words we gather all this information and establish our expectations. We know that we are not reading a newspaper article or a novel but a fairy tale, and we can calibrate our expectations accordingly.

Bonus Activity:

Ask participants to brainstorm different symbols that populate our world. Challenge them to list as many as possible in two minutes. Make sure to include less obvious symbols like letters, words, and street signs. Reflect on how we learn to "read" these signs and symbols. Ask individuals to share moments when they have been confused by a new symbol or by an old symbol in a new context.

SESSION ONE

Bonus Activity:
If one or more group members have traveled internationally, invite them to share some of their experiences getting adjusted to new symbols in a different place. How did they learn what these signs and symbols meant? How did it feel to be in a place where signs and symbols were not always clear to them?

Tip:
Martin Luther was certainly not the first Christian to have questions about the place of Revelation within Scripture. While the Gospels and many of Paul's letters were accepted as scriptural rather early on, texts like Revelation and Hebrews, for example, had a more difficult time gaining universal acceptance.

Bonus Activity:
The foreword to Revelation by Martin Luther can be found online at www.bible-researcher.com/antilegomena.html. Print it out to share with the group, and reflect on ways participants do or do not share Luther's concerns about Revelation.

Tip:
Encourage participants to think about Revelation not as a puzzle to be solved but as a theological reflection of hope in the midst of hopelessness. The aim of reading Revelation as the word of God is not to identify correctly who or what each character or symbol is supposed to represent, but what the book might teach us about God and lives lived in obedience to God.

Bonus Activity:
Ask participants to re-create in writing or in art an experience where they felt the presence of God in a particularly powerful way. As some share their efforts, ask all the participants to reflect on what emotions, experiences, or insights were most difficult to communicate.

Lutheran Context

1. Though his views eventually tempered, Martin Luther once wrote about Revelation, "My spirit cannot accommodate itself to this book. . . . Therefore I stick to the books which present Christ to me clearly and purely" (Preface to the Revelation of St. John, 1522, *Luther's Works*, ed. E. Theodore Bachmann [Fortress Press, 1960], 35:399). Luther was concerned initially that Revelation was too fantastical, too full of difficult symbols to be part of Scripture.

- In what ways do you think Luther's initial views about this book are correct? Discuss your general impressions of Revelation. Is this a book you or others in your group have read in the past? How often have you heard sermons on Revelation?

2. Though some Christians do not spend a great deal of time reading and reflecting on Revelation, many others do, and we can see and hear a variety of interpretations of Revelation in the wider culture.

- List some books, films, and TV shows dealing with Revelation or the end of the world. What do you find compelling or not compelling about these interpretations? As we continue this study, consider in what ways Revelation can help us think about God, our faith, and the world around us.

- Identify some songs dealing with Revelation or the end of the world. (See hymns 433–441 in ELW for ideas.) How is the end time interpreted in the music or lyrics?

Devotional Context

1. If you were to one day find yourself "in the spirit on the Lord's day" (1:10), what would you hope to learn about God and God's hope for the world?

2. Perhaps you haven't seen a vision of Jesus in full regalia or caught a glimpse into the end of the world as we know it. But have you ever experienced a moment like the one John describes in the opening verses of Revelation?

- Think about a time you were "in the spirit" or felt particularly at peace in the presence of God. How would you describe this moment in writing? What, if anything, would be difficult to put into words?

3. For John and his original readers, life under the power of Rome meant the constant threat of persecution. They looked to God's power over Roman might for the hope that God and God's people would prevail in the end.

SESSION ONE

- Discuss the hopes you have and what you look to for hope. How does this compare with the kind of hope John describes in Revelation?

Wrap-up

1. If there are any questions to explore further, write them on chart paper or a whiteboard. Ask for volunteers to do further research to share with the group at the next session.

2. Encourage participants to engage the daily readings. Explain that the sessions can only cover a portion of Revelation and that the daily readings help provide a wider context for discussion. Encourage participants to use a journal, computer, or smartphone to keep notes about questions and insights they gather as they read and reflect on the study.

3. Ask participants to share what big questions they hope to answer during this eight-session study. What are their goals and hopes for the study? Consider collecting these big questions and returning to them at the end of the eight sessions.

Tip:
Remind everyone that when reading a complex book like Revelation, many questions are bound to arise.

Pray

O God,
you raised up Jesus Christ
as your faithful witness and the first-born of the dead.
By your Holy Spirit, help us to witness to him
so that those who have not yet seen
may come to believe in him
who is, and was, and is to come. Amen.
(*Revised Common Lectionary Prayers*, Augsburg Fortress, 2002)

Tip:
Your group may want to keep the conversation going throughout the week. Consider creating an e-mail list, Facebook page, or private blog for the group.

Extending the Conversation (5 minutes)

Homework

1. Read the next session's Bible text: Revelation 2:12-17; 3:14-22.

2. Consider collecting a journal or scrapbook of experiences, conversations, news clippings, pop cultural references, and so on that ponder, portray, or draw upon images about the end of the world. As you collect these items, ask yourself what effect such discussions and images have on your sense of hope.

3. How do you picture Jesus in your mind? Take some time this week to create a few sketches. First, sketch out Jesus as described in Revelation 1:12-16. Next, sketch out Jesus as you picture him in your daily life. Last, do an online search for portraits of Jesus.

SESSION ONE

What differences and similarities do you note between the various images of Jesus? How do images of Jesus influence faith?

Enrichment

1. If you wish to read through the entire book of Revelation during this unit, read chapters 1–3 this week.

2. Hollywood movies about the end of the world or apocalypse are common. Of course, some of these movies aren't exactly works of art, but they do reflect something significant about contemporary culture. Every session of this study on Revelation will include a list of films you may want to watch (or watch again). As you view these films, ask yourself why we as a culture find these movies so compelling and watchable. What anxieties and fears, hopes and expectations do they reflect from our wider culture? This week, let's focus on two blockbuster films from 1998. That summer two different movies, *Armageddon* (Touchstone) and *Deep Impact* (Paramount), found creative ways to destroy the world and yet preserve human life. Why do you think these two very similar movies were released in the summer of 1998? What has changed between 1998 and today?

Tip: Each session will include one or two suggested films along with some discussion questions. Consider hosting a movie night at some point during the eight-session study to foster more conversation.

Tip: Sensitivities can vary from person to person. Encourage everyone to do some research on the content and theme of suggested movies prior to watching them. Also, feel free to brainstorm a list of alternative movies you might watch.

For Further Reading

The Rapture Exposed: The Message of Hope in the Book of Revelation, by Barbara Rossing. New York: Basic Books, 2004.

Revelation: A Commentary, by Brian K. Blount, in The New Testament Library. Louisville, KY: Westminster John Knox Press, 2009, pp. 1–23.

Revelation and the End of All Things, by Craig R. Koester. Grand Rapids, MI: Eerdmans, 2001.

Looking Ahead

1. Read the next session's Bible text: Revelation 2:12-17; 3:14-22.

2. Read through the Leader Guide for the next session and mark portions you wish to highlight for the group.

3. Make a checklist of any materials you'll need to do the Bonus Activities.

4. Pray for members of your group during the week.

5. Be on the lookout for current events (whether in politics or pop culture) that might inform the group's reading of Revelation.

SESSION TWO

Revelation 2:12-17; 3:14-22

Leader Session Guide

Life and Faith in Pergamum and Laodicea

Session Preparation

Before You Begin . . .

The letters to the seven churches are easily forgotten in light of what's coming next in Revelation. After all, doesn't it make sense that our attention would turn more quickly to the heavenly visions and ghastly images of later chapters rather than to these prosaic words at the beginning? However, these seven letters are crucial to our understanding of Revelation. They help remind us that Revelation was written to a very specific group of churches that had struggles and successes to which many of us today can relate.

Session Instructions

1. Read this Session Guide completely and highlight or underline any portions you wish to emphasize with the group. Note any Bonus Activities you wish to do.

2. If you plan to do any special activities, check to see what materials you'll need, if any.

3. Have extra Bibles on hand in case a member of the group forgets to bring one.

Session Overview

This session focuses on two of seven messages contained in Revelation: the messages to believers at Pergamum and Laodicea. The greatest challenge in reading any of these messages is that we are reading someone else's mail! Think about how difficult this can be. We don't know much about the message's sender or recipients. Words or phrases that sound cryptic to us as outsiders may have been easily understood by the original audience. In what ways, then, can we think about "someone else's mail" as God's word for us today?

HISTORICAL CONTEXT

Ancient ruins have been preserved at Pergamum and Laodicea, and we can gain a great deal by examining the historical and physical sites of these cities. The remains can help us imagine ancient life in those places and get a better sense of the challenges each community faced.

Focus Statement

The earliest Christians faced challenges both great and small, as we see in messages to seven churches in Revelation 3–4. In the message to believers in Pergamum, Revelation details what it means to live out Christian faith in the face of opposition and persecution. In contrast, Revelation chastises believers in Laodicea for the ambivalence of their faith and urges them to live into God's call.

Key Verses

"I know where you are living, where Satan's throne is. Yet you are holding fast to my name, and you did not deny your faith in me."
Revelation 2:13a

"I know your works; you are neither cold nor hot."
Revelation 3:15a

Focus Image

Message ©iStockphoto.com / Павел Игнатов

SESSION TWO

Zeus:
Known as Jupiter in Roman cultures, Zeus was believed to be the father of the whole pantheon of the gods, as well as all people. He served as a model for the patriarchs or male leaders of Greek and Roman households.

Nicolaitans:
The only references we have to this sect are found in Revelation 2:6 and 15, where they are rejected by Jesus. Their presence in both Ephesus and Pergamum may suggest their wide influence. In addition, some scholars see parallels in the teaching of "Jezebel" in 2:20-25 and the condemnation of the Nicolaitans in 2:15. Was "Jezebel" perhaps also a Nicolaitan?

Manna:
Manna was the heavenly food provided by God to the Israelites while they wandered the wilderness after leaving Egypt (see Exodus 16:4). It became a symbol of God's eternal sustenance of God's people as well as a harbinger of the last days.

In the end, both cities had their gifts and curses. Pergamum was set in a beautiful location but was also a center of persecution. The presence of an altar to **Zeus** on the acropolis—that is, in a most prominent location in the city—was a daily reminder for Christians that they were in constant danger. Laodicea was a place of wealth and extravagance. The Christians there apparently shared in that abundance but in doing so lost sight of their reliance on God for all things.

In both cases, elements of the local topography help shape the letter. "Satan's throne" in the message to Pergamum may have referred to the temple of Zeus. The image of tepid water in the message to Laodicea probably evoked the hot springs in nearby Hierapolis that supplied water to the city.

Why are these city features important? Think about New York or Washington, London or Paris, Cairo or Baghdad. What images come to mind? Often we associate these places with particular features that reflect what life in that city is like.

Literary Context

The letters to Pergamum and Laodicea contain references to local and biblical images that may not be familiar to us. One key in teaching this material is becoming comfortable with what we do not know and perhaps cannot know. For example, the exact character of the **Nicolaitans** may be lost to history. Moreover, exactly what Revelation means by the "hidden **manna**" and "white stone" of 2:17 may never become evident to us. At the same time, the underlying themes of these messages can be discerned if we read carefully.

Let the contrast between the two letters help instruct your group. The different tones of the messages can help make sense of the particularities of each. The nurturing tone of the message to Pergamum goes to believers in need of encouragement in the midst of great persecution and the temptation to desert the gospel. We may not know who the Nicolaitans were exactly, but we can imagine the temptation to leave God's path. We may not understand fully the images of 2:17, but we too can find comfort in God's ever-present care for us in the midst of life's challenges.

In sharp contrast to this, we have the corrective message to Laodicea. Here, the images of gold, white robes, and salve may cause some confusion. Encourage participants to think of things today that help us feel comfortable, secure, and well. Then have them consider whether our reliance on these things might interfere with our relationship with God.

Lutheran Context

The image of Jesus knocking on a door may be familiar to your group. A depiction of it may even be hanging somewhere on the walls of your church. There is a comfort in the soft knocking of Jesus on the door. But there is also a sense of judgment in this image in our text. Reading the wider context of the message to Laodicea helps bring out the many dimensions of this powerful image. It is meant to be comforting but also confrontational. The Christians in Laodicea were in need of redirection; they had lost their way. For Lutherans, law and gospel are not opposites or contradictions; they function together to help reveal the gospel of Christ. In this case, the good news of Jesus' presence in our lives is also law.

Furthermore, Lutherans also confess that Scripture interprets Scripture, that one Bible text may help us to understand another Bible text. This is particularly true in the case of the messages to the seven churches in Revelation. These seven letters give us a unique opportunity to get a glimpse into the lives of Christian communities in the ancient world. By considering what they may have meant for the original audiences, we can come to a better understanding of how they continue to address us today.

Revelation probably always began with this collection of messages. Perhaps in doing this, the author wanted to make Revelation both cosmic and local, universal and particular. Revelation teaches that even as we struggle in our individual contexts, we are bound together with fellow believers around the world and with God's cosmic plan for the world.

Devotional Context

How can someone else's mail inspire us? In the case of these two messages with two very different tones, we are reminded of the very different challenges believers and churches have faced in the past and continue to deal with today. How do we find comfort in the midst of trouble? How is God calling us to reassess how we live individually and communally?

Some Christians in North America worry that they are being persecuted. This may be true to an extent, but the experience of the Christians in Pergamum as well as our sisters and brothers around the world today ought to cause us to take pause. What is

SESSION TWO

the nature of oppression? What is the difference between mere inconveniences and life-threatening persecution?

At the same time, even those who experience a great deal of comfort can face many challenges and obstacles. Like the Christians in Laodicea, they need to hear that the "hidden manna," God's eternal provision, is with them and their names have been written on the "white stone." God does not forget us in our distress. The message to Laodicea also raises this question: Have we grown too accustomed to those things that make us wealthy and well?

Facilitator's Prayer

God of all creation, meet us in our sorrows and walk with us in our distress. Open our eyes to walk alongside those who suffer and recognize their oppression. Grant us mercy, God, when we fall short, when we lean on the things of this world to provide what only you can give. Amen.

Gather (10–15 minutes)

Check-in

Invite learners to share completed homework or any new thoughts or insights about the last session. Be ready to give a brief recap of that session if necessary.

Tip: Spend a few minutes summarizing last week's session but also allow space for participants to share what they thought about in the intervening week. Did Revelation come up in any unexpected ways in the course of the week?

Pray

God, thank you for meeting us in the midst of our joys and our sorrows, our successes and our failures. Walk with us now as we open your word. Join us as we struggle to live out your call. Help us as we read together. Amen.

Tip: Make time during these moments of prayer for individuals to share their prayer concerns. This will provide an opportunity to connect the cosmic vision of Revelation to our everyday concerns as believers. What Revelation is finally about is God's care for each and every one of us.

Focus Activity

Take a look at the Focus Image. Imagine that your congregation has received a message from a trusted leader who knows you well. What might this person say about your church? What are your strengths and challenges? What is the main point of the message likely to be? Would your congregation be receptive to both correction and praise?

Tip: Another way to frame the Focus Activity is to have the group imagine what Jesus, Paul, or the author of Revelation might write to your congregation. Have participants share their ideas with two or three others in the group.

SESSION TWO

Open Scripture (10–15 minutes)

To emphasize the different tones of the two letters, have one person read the letter to Pergamum (2:12-17) and another read the letter to Laodicea (3:14-22). Think about the individuals in your group when you choose these readers. Consider asking someone with a nurturing voice to read the first letter, and someone with a more strict voice to read the second letter.

Conduct a quick poll after the letters are read, asking participants which letter they would rather receive.

Read Revelation 2:12-17; 3:14-22; two of the seven letters imbedded in Revelation 3–4.

- The tone of these two messages is strikingly different. Which would you rather receive? Why?
- What might help you better understand these two messages?
- What questions arise for you as you listen to these texts?

Join the Conversation (25–55 minutes)

Historical Context

1. Knowing something about the ancient cities of Pergamum and Laodicea will help us read the session texts. Locate Pergamum and Laodicea on the map below.

Pergamum was and is a beautiful site. Located on the Aegean Sea, the area is dominated by an elevated area where the city's

 Tip:
Consider asking a man to read the encouraging letter of Pergamum, and a woman to read the more authoritative letter to Laodicea. How do these choices affect the way the group hears the tone of the letters?

 Tip:
Do an online search for high-quality images of Pergamum, Laodicea, and/or the other cities that received messages in Revelation. Project these pictures for the group to see.

 Bonus Activity:
Have groups of two or three pick a large city today (for example, New York, London, or Beijing). What images and ideas might the author of Revelation have used in writing messages to people here? What city features might be used to address issues of faith and life?

 Bonus Activity:
Lead the group in drafting a letter in response to the author of Revelation from the perspective of Christians in Pergamum or Laodicea. How would you have received the letter? What questions would you still have?

Session 2: Revelation 2:12-17; 3:14-22   23

most important religious and political structures stood. A huge ancient theater was even built into the side of this acropolis. And yet this beautiful setting was a difficult one for the Christians in Pergamum. Revelation cites a number of difficulties they face, one of which is the presence of "Satan's throne." What does the author of Revelation mean by this? We can't be entirely sure. It could refer to the judicial seat that condemned Antipas (see 2:13), to Pergamum's involvement in the imperial cult, or to a massive altar dedicated to Zeus, with remains we can still see in Pergamum.

- Refer to the first photo below. Imagine for a moment attending a performance of a play in ancient times, seated on the side of the hill overlooking the surrounding area. What would that have been like?
- Take a look at the photos on this page from Pergamum. Describe what life might have been like for Christians in this city, in light of these photos and Revelation 2:12-17.

Remains of theater in Pergamum.

A view from the Acropolis in Pergamum.

Remains of the Altar to Zeus in Pergamum.

Hot springs in Hierapolis, near Laodicea.

SESSION TWO

2. Laodicea sat at an important economic crossroads. Two ancient highways met at the city, making it a center of commerce. This prominent location assured general prosperity among the local residents. In fact, not even a devastating earthquake in 60 C.E. could restrain Laodicea's success; the locals even rejected financial help from Rome as they rebuilt. What evidence of Laodicea's wealth do you see in Revelation 3:14-22?

- Despite Laodicea's prosperity, water had to be imported from hot springs in the nearby city of Hierapolis. (See photo on the previous page.) By the time the warm water reached Laodicea, it was tepid and full of minerals—not exactly a refreshing drink. How might this fact help you better understand Revelation 3:15-16?

Literary Context

1. In the message to Pergamum, the writer of Revelation mentions four names that were probably familiar to believers in that city.

- Review Revelation 2:13. What do we learn here about Antipas? What does his death mean for the rest of the community of believers?

- Read Revelation 2:14. Balaam was known for being obstinate before God. God finally grew so frustrated that God literally spoke through Balaam's donkey. Find out more about the prophet Balaam and Balak, king of Moab, by reading Numbers 22–24 and 31:15 as well as 2 Peter 2:15-16 and Jude 11. What did Balaam do that was so wrong that, many years later, Revelation would use him as an example of faithlessness? What does the allusion to Balaam and Balak mean for early Christians in Pergamum?

- Read Revelation 2:6, 15. Besides these brief mentions in Revelation, we don't know much about the Nicolaitans. What might we discern about them from these passages? What does the presence of this sect mean for the community in Pergamum?

2. Review the message to Laodicea, Revelation 3:14-22.

- Discuss the similarities and differences between this letter and the one to Pergamum.

- Notice the rich images Revelation uses in 3:17-18. Which stand out to you? In what way does the refined gold make people who already think they are rich truly rich? In what ways do the white robes make people who already think they dress in fine clothing truly prosperous? In what ways does a salve make people who already think they are healthy truly whole?

Tip:
If you wish to spend some time talking about Balaam, make sure you read Numbers 22–24 in advance. During the session, it may work best for you to summarize and retell this story.

Bonus Activity:
Read another of the seven letters found in Revelation 3–4 in advance. Share the letter and lead a discussion about how this letter is similar to and different from the letters to Pergamum and Laodicea.

Bonus Activity:
Using only the text of another letter found in Revelation 3–4, invite participants to draw a visual depiction of the city being addressed. Discuss how easy or difficult this is to do.

SESSION TWO

 Bonus Activity:
Do an online search for images depicting Jesus knocking on the door. Print or project these images for your group. Discuss: In what ways do these pieces of art faithfully represent Revelation 3:20? In what ways do they fall short? Where do you see law and gospel in these images?

 Bonus Activity:
If your group is large enough, have participants form five groups. Assign each group one of the other messages in Revelation 2–3 to read and compare to the letters to Pergamum and Laodicea. Give each group some time to report their findings to the large group. What new insights emerge from this activity?

 Tip:
As participants reflect on the privileges afforded to them and the difficulties many Christians face around the world, help them think of ways to put their faith into action. Encourage them to support and pray for the work of organizations like Lutheran Social Services, Lutheran World Relief, and International Justice Mission. Also discuss what your congregation can do to support efforts like these.

 Bonus Activity:
Find a recent news story about the persecution of Christians outside North America. Print out or project the article for all to read. What does the suffering of Christians around the world mean for us? How can we help? How should we respond?

Lutheran Context

1. Central to how Lutherans read Scripture is the understanding that God's word speaks both law and gospel, judgment and salvation. We see both present in the messages we read today.

- Let's focus on one image in particular, of Jesus knocking at a door (3:20). Considering what comes before verse 20, in what ways is the image of Jesus knocking both law *and* gospel? How is this image a reminder of Jesus reaching out to us in love? How is it a reminder of our brokenness?

2. Lutherans are also guided in reading the Bible by the principle *Scripture interprets Scripture.* Rather than reading and interpreting passages in isolation, we look at related passages and at Scripture as a whole. If we read only one of the messages to the churches in Revelation, we might not see a full picture of the many ways Christians thrived and struggled in the earliest days of the church and still today.

- What do we learn when we read Revelation 2:12-17 and 3:14-22 together that we could not learn by reading either letter by itself?

Devotional Context

1. For some Christians in antiquity, perhaps like those in Pergamum, persecution was a daily reality. For some Christians today this is still the case, and practicing their faith is a risk they must choose to take each day. How does Revelation speak to Christians struggling under the burden of oppression?

2. "I am rich, I have prospered, and I need nothing" (3:17a), the people in Laodicea said, but the message to them in Revelation is a powerful reminder that external appearances do not always coincide with internal realities. Many of us might look composed on the outside, even as our families are falling apart. Many of us might have the newest stuff, while our bank accounts dwindle. In what ways do you see in yourself the outward confidence but inward brokenness of the Laodiceans? How does Revelation speak to this situation?

SESSION TWO

Wrap-up

1. If there are any questions to explore further, write them on chart paper or a whiteboard. Ask for volunteers to do further research to share with the group at the next session.

2. Encourage participants to pick one of the other messages in Revelation 2 and 3 to study deeply during this week. Using the Internet and other resources, how much can we learn about these places and what they look like today?

Pray

God, thank you for your Word. Thank you for the words of life we find there. Help us to see you in the face of the suffering and persecuted. Drive us to their aid. Let us not take our advantages for granted but use them to your glory. Amen.

Tip:
Remind participants that the word of God can meet us in unexpected ways. Encourage them to discern ways in which Revelation emerges in daily conversations, evening newscasts, and our contemplation. Such insights are vital to the work of studying Scripture. Encourage participants to bring these insights to your shared study of the Bible.

Extending the Conversation (5 minutes)

Homework

1. Read the next session's Bible text: Revelation 4:1-6a; 5:1-10.

2. Take a virtual tour of the seven cities addressed in Revelation at www2.luthersem.edu/ckoester/revelation/main.htm. Consider talking with someone who has visited these sites in Turkey, or take a trip to see them in person. Travel agencies are often willing to make arrangements for church groups to travel to these locations.

3. Write a message to your church, modeling your message after those found in Revelation. What words of encouragement does your church need to hear today? In what ways should your church take a different path? How might Jesus encourage your congregation today?

Enrichment

1. If you wish to read through the entire book of Revelation during this unit, read chapters 4-5 this week.

2. Apocalyptic movies are not always as dramatic or explosive as the films listed in the session 1 Enrichment section. Sometimes the end of the world as we know it can be subtler but no less pernicious and destructive. Watch *Wall-E* (Disney/Pixar, 2008) this week. The movie received a well-deserved Oscar nomination, and seeing it together will generate a great deal of conversation.

Tip:
The movie *Wall-E* is very family-friendly. Consider having an intergenerational movie night. Encourage parents to bring their children, grandparents to bring their grandchildren, aunts and uncles to bring their nieces and nephews. Discover that sometimes—even often—the minds of children grasp deep matters better than adults!

SESSION TWO

Tip:
In the book *The Lost Letters of Pergamum: A Story from the New Testament World* (Baker Academic, 2002), Bruce W. Longenecker provides a fictional correspondence between Luke and the Antipas mentioned in Revelation. At the same time, he teaches the reader a great deal about ancient contexts. Consider leading a book study on this novelization of the biblical text.

Once again, wonder together whether this movie reflects anxieties and fears, hopes and expectations that exist in our wider culture. In what ways do we worry that our demise may come from within us, rather than from outside us? In what ways can we interpret *Wall-E* as a message to today's churches, akin to the seven messages in Revelation?

For Further Reading

"Coming Out of Babylon: A First-World Reading of Revelation among Immigrants," by Harry O. Maier, in *From Every People and Nation: The Book of Revelation*, ed. David Rhoads. Minneapolis: Fortress Press, 2005, pp. 62–81.

The Lost Letters of Pergamum: A Story from the New Testament World, by Bruce W. Longenecker. Grand Rapids, MI: Baker Academic, 2002.

Reading Revelation Responsibly: Uncivil Worship and Witness; Following the Lamb into the New Creation, by Michael J. Gorman. Eugene, OR: Cascade Books, 2011. See especially pp. 81–101.

Looking Ahead

1. Read the next session's Bible text: Revelation 4:1-6a; 5:1-10.

2. Read through the Leader Guide for the next session and mark portions you wish to highlight for the group.

3. Make a checklist of any materials you'll need to do the Bonus Activities.

4. Pray for members of your group during the week.

SESSION THREE

Revelation 4:1-6a; 5:1-10

Leader Session Guide

Visions of God and the Lamb

Session Preparation

Before You Begin . . .

A number of biblical scholars concur that chapters 4 and 5 are at the very center of Revelation's theology and perspective. We are easily distracted by the many woes and powerful imagery that follow in later chapters, but it is the might of God, exemplified in the lamb that was slain, that helps make sense of this enigmatic book. God is great and worthy of worship. God also cares for us profoundly, as we see in Jesus' sacrifice.

Session Instructions

1. Read this Session Guide completely and highlight or underline any portions you wish to emphasize with the group. Note any Bonus Activities you wish to do.

2. If you plan to do any special activities, check to see what materials you'll need, if any.

3. Have extra Bibles on hand in case a member of the group forgets to bring one.

Session Overview

Chapters 4 and 5 may be the most important ones in Revelation. In the description of the mighty God and powerful Lion—who is also a slaughtered Lamb—we see the very foundation of Revelation's hopes. In the end, it is not the trauma of tribulation or the victory of the victims of history that motivates the author of Revelation. Instead, it is an unswerving belief in God and Christ that makes sense of both the tribulations and the victories that will be recorded in subsequent chapters.

HISTORICAL CONTEXT

Two dominant images in our texts relate to the ancient world in important ways: the throne room of God and the scroll with seven seals. Notice that Revelation talks about a "throne room" but avoids directly describing God. In fact, it talks about God only with similes and symbols. Why is this? In abiding by the commandment, "You shall not make wrongful use of the name of the LORD your God, for the LORD will not acquit anyone who misuses his name" (Exodus 20:7), Jews in the ancient world avoided speaking the name of God. And in seeking to avoid the sin of idolatry, Jews in the ancient world avoided embodying God in any particular way. The Hebrew Bible further states that seeing

Focus Statement

Drawn into the very presence of God, the author of Revelation can only appeal to lofty and enigmatic language. While the God of Revelation is exalted in the highest heavens, this same God is also profoundly concerned with the plight of God's children.

Key Verses

After this I looked, and there in heaven a door stood open! Revelation 4:1a

"See, the Lion of the tribe of Judah, the Root of David, has conquered, so that he can open the scroll and its seven seals." Revelation 5:5b

Focus Image

Revelation by Jim LePage (jimlepage.com)

SESSION THREE

> **? Seven:**
> The number seven is closely associated with God and divine matters throughout the book of Revelation. It symbolizes completeness. For example, it is no accident that there are seven churches addressed in the opening chapters of Revelation. By addressing exactly *seven* churches, all churches are symbolically addressed.

> **? Twenty-four elders:**
> The identity of the twenty-four elders is a matter of some debate among scholars. This could be an allusion to the twelve tribes of Israel and the twelve disciples. More important than who they are, however, is *how* they act. They have crowns symbolizing their honor, but they willingly and freely lay down their crowns in worship of God. Indeed, their only function in all of Revelation is praise and worship of God! (See 5:8-10; 11:16; 19:4.)

the face of God means instant death. In Revelation, God is too holy for mere words. God cannot be depicted like so many idols. So the description of God in Revelation 4 is indirect. God is "one seated on the throne" who "looks like jasper and carnelian" (4:2-3). (Precious elements like these are also used in Ezekiel 1:16, 26, and 27 to emphasize God's splendor.) The only proper response to such splendor is worship, as the twenty-four elders demonstrate.

The second image is the scroll with **seven** seals. Messages were sealed with wax in the ancient world to ensure that they were only read by designated recipients. A broken or disturbed seal was evidence that someone else had already read the message. The presence of *seven* seals is significant for two reasons. First, the number seven calls us back to the many times this number has already appeared in the book. God is associated with the number seven and thus this message comes from a divine source. Second, the seven seals ensure that the message can only be opened by its proper recipient: the Lamb! Without the Lamb, the revelation could not be known.

Literary Context

One of the challenges in reading these texts is the density of their symbolism. Who are the **twenty-four elders**? What do their crowns represent? To these and other questions, scholars have provided a number of answers. Because we could easily get stuck trying to resolve all these issues, this session will use another approach to this material.

There are two overarching themes in Revelation 4–5: the character of God and the character of God's servant, who is able to unveil God's plan for God's people yesterday, today, and forever. God is a God of majesty and power. God puts to shame the supposed "kings" of the earth. As these kings sit on thrones adorned by spoils gained in war and conquest, God sits on a much greater throne gained simply because of who God is.

Who then is God's servant? He is a fierce lion but also a meek lamb. In Christ, we see the bringing together of power and weakness in a way that challenges our usual views. Both in antiquity and today, power is typically wielded by those willing to engage in violence, those willing to go to any ends to maintain their position. Every once in a while, however, power comes through what we normally would call weakness. In what ways have towering figures in history like Gandhi, Mother Teresa, and Martin Luther King Jr. embraced this paradoxical alignment of power and weakness?

SESSION THREE

LUTHERAN CONTEXT

God and Christ are the central figures of these two chapters. The rest of the cast of characters appear only to point to God and Christ, acknowledge their love for humanity, and worship for all eternity. While God and Christ are, of course, central to our faith, these passages call us to stretch our theological imagination. They may even draw us to places of some discomfort. The aim in this section of the study, therefore, is to help participants think deeply and widely about two central confessions: God is great, mighty, and powerful; Christ is victorious through weakness and powerful through sacrifice.

How we picture God is fundamental to our faith. Because we tend not to have many artistic depictions of God in many of our churches, we are often stuck with thoughts of a bearded old man. One of our aims in reading Revelation 4 is to stretch our imagination about God beyond these simple caricatures.

In contrast, many church buildings display images of Jesus, yet these images do not always stretch our imagination. The contrast in Revelation 5 between the victorious lion and the slaughtered lamb is an ideal place to begin thinking about Jesus beyond the usual depictions.

DEVOTIONAL CONTEXT

God and Christ are the central characters here, but we would be mistaken to assume that we who are followers of Christ are absent from these heavenly scenes. How do we fit into these fantastic narratives of the heavenly throne room?

We can see ourselves in the twenty-four elders. In Revelation 2:10, the Christians of Smyrna are promised crowns if they remain faithful even to death. In Revelation 3:11, the believers in Philadelphia are admonished to remain faithful lest they lose their crowns. Similarly, in Revelation 3:4-5, the believers in Sardis are promised white robes "if you conquer," and in Revelation 3:18, the Laodiceans are offered white robes. The twenty-four elders wear the heavenly rewards of their faithfulness.

But to what end are the elders so finely adorned? It is not for their own sake, in the end, but for God's. Their primary function is to worship, casting aside their crowns as they bow before God and Christ alike.

SESSION THREE

Therefore, help draw participants into the drama in the heavenly throne room and help them see that ordinary, everyday lives can be led in the shadow of God's glory. Ultimately, you don't need to be transported into heaven to be in God's presence.

Facilitator's Prayer

Pray the prayers of Revelation 4:

"Holy, holy, holy, the Lord God the Almighty, who was and is and is to come." (Revelation 4:8b)

"You are worthy, our Lord and God, to receive glory and honor and power, for you created all things, and by your will they existed and were created." (Revelation 4:11)

Gather (10-15 minutes)

Check-in

Invite learners to share completed homework or any new thoughts or insights about the last session. Be ready to give a brief recap of that session if necessary.

Pray

*Mighty God,
in whom we know the power of redemption,
you stand among us in the shadows of our time.
As we move through every sorrow and trial of this life,
uphold us with knowledge of the final morning
when, in the glorious presence of your risen Son,
we will share in his resurrection,
redeemed and restored to the fullness of life
and forever freed to be your people. Amen.*
(*Revised Common Lectionary Prayers*, Augsburg Fortress, 2002)

Focus Activity

Take a look at the Focus Image. The artist has created a series of pieces trying to encapsulate each biblical book with one arresting image. What do you think of his effort to summarize Revelation here? What might it suggest about Revelation that its most important image is not one of dragons or a dark horse, but the lamb that was slain? So far in your study of Revelation, what to you is the most important image or idea?

 Tip:
If new people join the Bible study this week, spend a few minutes as you check in to review where you've been. For example, ask participants to name the most important insights they've gained in the first couple of weeks of study, and list questions they still have.

Tip:
Revelation includes a number of prayers and songs of praise. Draw on their language as you compose your own prayers. Reflect together with the group on how the words of Scripture can and should shape our times of prayer.

Tip:
Do an online search for other images related to Revelation. What do these images teach us about how Revelation is perceived in our culture?

SESSION THREE

Open Scripture (10–15 minutes)

As you read these texts out loud, invite participants to listen with their eyes closed and imagine the scene. Then ask participants to identify one or two things that stood out to them during this reading.

OR

Assign different "parts" to various participants to read, such as narrator, "the first voice" in 4:1, four individuals as the four living creatures, several individuals as the elders, and "a mighty angel." Encourage participants to imagine the scene from these different perspectives.

Read Revelation 4:1-6a; 5:1-10.
- What gives you hope in these texts?
- What do you find puzzling?
- How would you describe these texts?

 Tip:
Encourage your pastor and other worship leaders to incorporate readings of Revelation in Sunday morning worship. Hearing these texts both in Bible study and in worship will invite deeper reflection on these texts.

Join the Conversation (25–55 minutes)

Historical Context

1. Revelation's second set of visions begins in chapter 4. It seems as if words fail as the writer tries to describe the experience of being brought into God's throne room.

- Read Revelation 4:1-6a again. In a world where Rome was the supreme power, the description of God here is deeply political. God's throne room is not just equal to that of Caesar but far exceeds it in beauty and splendor. God's power is so great that lightning and thunder answer to it. How might this portrait of God speak to the powerful today?

- What other primary characteristics of God are detailed in Revelation 4:1-6a? What does this description tell us about God and how we ought to live today?

2. One of the more powerful symbols in Revelation 5 is the image of the scroll with seven seals. The number seven, which represented perfection in the ancient world, is repeated many times in this book (see Revelation 1:20, for example). In Revelation, this number is tied to God and God's work in powerful ways. It is not part of a secret code but rather a shorthand way of declaring God's attributes. The seven seals on the scroll assure that only the right individual will open these

 Tip:
Many sources on Revelation dwell on trying to determine the precise meaning of the symbols, but spend little time on the more important theological points in the text. It is worth saying again that in the study of Revelation it is best not to miss the forest for the trees. Encourage individuals wishing to dig deeper into Revelation's symbolism to take a look at the books and commentaries listed at the end of each session. Consider having available a few copies of these resources.

 Bonus Activity:
Provide art supplies and invite participants to draw, paint, storyboard, or sketch some portion of the readings they found particularly striking. These texts are meant to evoke images in our minds as we read and hear them. Allow time for participants to share their work with one another. What role does imagination play in our faith?

Session 3: Revelation 4:1-6a; 5:1-10   33

SESSION THREE

 Bonus Activity:
The contents of the scroll with seven seals will be unveiled in subsequent chapters of Revelation. This scroll is described as containing the world's most valuable information—information so vital that only Christ himself can reveal it. Discuss: What kind of message would you want to hear from God? What questions would you have asked in the throne room of God? What is the most valuable information in the world today?

 Bonus Activity:
Looking at Scripture from a literary perspective can involve studying how a particular word or phrase is used. Do a quick word study on the frequency and location of the number seven in Revelation. (Use a concordance or search an online or electronic version of the Bible.) Have volunteers read several of the passages, and discuss how and when the number is used. Is it connected to someone or something? What does it seem to mean?

 Tip:
Luther imagined the texts of Scripture as straw in the manger of the Christ child. Asking what shows forth Christ in a text means asking questions such as these: How does this text prepare us to meet Christ? How does it lead us to understand, worship, and serve Christ more deeply?

 Bonus Activity:
Develop and implement a brief worship service using the imagery and words of Revelation 4–5. You could design a liturgy using songs and prayers from these chapters. Alternatively, you could create a brief worship experience with members of the group that would emulate the worship of the elders.

---

previously unknown plans. In the ancient world, a seal was like securely closing an envelope. An intact seal meant the contents of the message had been safely guarded and no one else had read the message on the scroll.

- In the end, what is it that makes the Lamb worthy of opening this scroll?

Literary Context

1. There is a literary shift from the messages of Revelation 2 and 3 to the vision that begins in chapter 4. And yet these chapters are also connected.

- Read Revelation 3:20-22 and 4:1-6a. How are these chapters drawn together?

2. It is easy to be distracted by the "fireworks" of Revelation, such as dragons and horsemen ready to consume the earth. However, these are not at the center of what the book is all about. Instead, in Revelation 4–5, we catch a glimpse of God's glory and Jesus' power through weakness. This is a sublime summary of Revelation's perspective and the truth that the book proclaims behind all the histrionics and eye-popping imagery.

Note the sharp contrast between 5:5 and 5:6. First, one of the elders comforts John by reminding him that "the Lion of the tribe of Judah . . . has conquered," and thus he alone can open the scroll. What then should we expect to see in the next verse? Certainly not a slaughtered lamb—yet that is precisely what John sees.

- Discuss how God's glory is a part of your faith. How can a God enthroned in the heavens be present in your everyday life?
- How is Jesus both Lion and Lamb in Revelation 5:1-10?

Lutheran Context

1. Any image of God we come up with will always somehow fall short. God is always beyond our words and our imaginations. At the same time, we try to understand God because how we imagine God shapes how we live our lives and how we relate to God.

- In your daily life, how do you picture or imagine God? How does your picture of God affect the way you live your life and relate to God?

2. Lutherans read Scripture looking for "what shows forth Christ." In other words, in what new and insightful ways does the Bible text we are reading point us to Christ? Let's ask this

question of Revelation 5. First Jesus is depicted as a lion, and then as a lamb. Moreover, the lamb has seven horns and seven eyes!

- Review the worship of the leaders in Revelation 5:9-10, then discuss how Revelation 5 reveals Christ to you in a new way.
- Sing "This Is the Feast" (ELW p. 101). How is Jesus depicted in this hymn?

Devotional Context

1. On a blank piece of paper, sketch out some symbols, images, or words that come to mind when you think about God. In what ways have these shifted during your life? What symbols, images, or words from Revelation resonate with how you think about God?

2. The new song that the twenty-four elders sing concludes, "You have made them to be a kingdom and priests serving our God, and they will reign on earth" (5:10).

- In what ways are you and fellow believers a kingdom? In what ways are you a priest?
- When most of us think about "reigning on earth," we think about someone exercising political and economic power. Discuss what kind of power and what kind of reign Revelation imagines.

Wrap-up

1. If there are any questions to explore further, write them on chart paper or a whiteboard. Ask for volunteers to do further research to share with the group at the next session.

2. When we think about God and Christ, who do we imagine they are?

3. What images of God and Jesus are present in the wider culture? How do these images shape us in both positive and negative ways?

Pray

God of glory, you have chosen to walk in our midst. For that we give you our thanks. God of might, you embraced weakness in order to make your love known to us. For that we give you our thanks. God of majesty, you are present with us whether our lives are full of joy or pain. For all these things we give you our worship and praise. Amen.

 Bonus Activity:
Talk about the function of art and images in our faith. What kind of art is found in your church building? What could newcomers learn about your congregation if all they saw was the art in your worship space or meeting areas? If possible, bring in some of these pieces of art or take a tour of your church to see the artwork displayed.

 Tip:
As you reflect on symbols, images, or words related to God, spend some time also thinking together about how we imagine Jesus. How do various images of Jesus help or hinder our faith?

 Bonus Activity:
Use the reading practice of "dwelling in the word" with Revelation 5:9-10. See more details at www.bookoffaith.org/dwelling.html.

 Tip:
Remind participants again how central and important Revelation 4 and 5 are to the rest of the book. It is these visions of God and Christ that help make sense of all the chaos and justice, violence and peace, destruction and restoration that will be narrated in the rest of Revelation.

SESSION THREE

Extending the Conversation (5 minutes)

Homework

1. Read the next session's Bible text: Revelation 6:15—7:17.

2. Create your own portrait of God's "throne room." What kind of place would be appropriate to host the God of the universe—a lofty and exalted place like a throne room, or a humbler locale like a manger? Reflect on what difference it makes to have different pictures of God in our minds.

3. Read Revelation 4:1-11 in one sitting, paying special attention to how the four living creatures and the elders react to God. What is the shape of their worship? How do they worship? What do they say? How are their bodies involved in worship? In light of Revelation 4, write a one-sentence definition of worship. Post it in a place where you will see it every day—on your refrigerator or on the bathroom mirror, for instance. Contemplate the nature and purpose of worship throughout the week. Be ready to share any new insights at the next session.

Enrichment

1. If you wish to read through the entire book of Revelation during this unit, read chapters 6-11 this week.

2. The film *Children of Men* (Universal, 2006) imagines our world twenty years in the future. In this world, universal infertility has created a deep sense of despair all over the world. The film depicts a sliver of hope in the midst of all this hopelessness. After viewing the film, reflect on the sources of hope and despair in our world today. What is the nature of hope in Revelation? In what ways does Revelation give you hope today? Also think about how nations and people exert power in the film and in today's world. How does God exercise power in Revelation and in your life?

SESSION THREE

For Further Reading

Revelation for Everyone, by N. T. Wright. Louisville, KY: Westminster John Knox Press, 2011.

What Does Revelation Really Reveal? Unlocking the Mystery, by Warren Carter. Nashville: Abingdon Press, 2011.

Looking Ahead

1. Read the next session's Bible text: Revelation 6:15—7:17.

2. Read through the Leader Guide for the next session and mark portions you wish to highlight for the group.

3. Make a checklist of any materials you'll need to do the Bonus Activities.

4. Pray for members of your group during the week.

Tip:
Consider following up this Bible study with two to four sessions digging into one of these books on Revelation.

SESSION FOUR

Revelation 6:15—7:17

Leader Session Guide

Focus Statement

Revelation's message travels along two paths. While ordeals, tribulations, and plagues characterize both the present and the future, God's promises are ever faithful even in the midst of these trials.

Key Verse

After this I looked, and there was a great multitude that no one could count, from every nation, from all tribes and peoples and languages, standing before the throne and before the Lamb, robed in white, with palm branches in their hands. Revelation 7:9

Focus Image

Albrecht Durer, *Four Horsemen of the Apocalypse*, ©iStockphoto.com / Darko Veselinovic

Destruction and Protection

Session Preparation

Before You Begin . . .

Troubles and tribulations will always test our faith. When life makes the least sense, trusting God can prove difficult. Scripture is full of the struggles of faithful people throughout the ages trying to understand God in the midst of crisis and loss. What challenges the faith of the people in your group? How can we express these challenges while also leaning on God's promises?

Session Instructions

1. Read this Session Guide completely and highlight or underline any portions you wish to emphasize with the group. Note any Bonus Activities you wish to do.

2. If you plan to do any special activities, check to see what materials you'll need, if any.

3. Have extra Bibles on hand in case a member of the group forgets to bring one.

Session Overview

Despite all the book's theatrics, Revelation is focused on God. In the session text, we see the complexities of God's relationship with us. God judges *and* shows mercy. God cares for us and marks us for salvation, even in the midst of tribulations. These are the central confessions of Revelation 6 and 7.

LITERARY CONTEXT

In the ancient world, which was marked by **economic limitations** and **political instability,** a comfortable and secure life was within reach for very few people. The author of Revelation knows intimately the disastrous effects natural and political forces could bring to bear on the Christian community. In a world like this, only one dream and only one hope could suffice.

The powerful will not be victorious in the end. The oppressed will be protected. Both of these things will be true, not because the faithful try hard enough or because the powerful self-destruct, but because God is a faithful and just judge, powerful and compassionate.

SESSION FOUR

The faithfulness of God is most pressing for us when we are most in need of God's care. But today it may be only when things fall apart that many of us remember how close we are to a life of disorder. For example, how many of us could have imagined that a disaster like Hurricane Katrina and its aftermath could strike an American city? How powerless did we feel as we watched news coverage of the Haitian earthquake from the comfort of our homes? Revelation shows us that we rely on God for all things and challenges us to remember this throughout our lives.

Historical Context

Think about how you would describe our current culture to someone who had never experienced it. Where would you start? What features of the culture would you highlight? One of the more difficult aspects of such an exercise would be putting into words things we normally take for granted. In the ancient world, the violence of life was precisely one of those cultural aspects one would take for granted. And in a world marked by violence, the author of Revelation uses the language and images of his time.

Part of what makes reading Revelation difficult is trying to hold together a God who promises grace and mercy but also breathes justice. Help the members of your group reflect together on these aspects of God's character. The tendency of many Christians is to focus on one aspect or another. Some Christians emphasize a God of judgment and wrath, preaching "hellfire and brimstone." Other Christians emphasize a God of grace and mercy, preaching that God is love. Revelation reminds us that both perspectives are correct *and* incomplete. We cannot fully understand God without embracing both of these aspects of God's character.

In addition, as you turn together to reflect on the 144,000 of Israel who are sealed, help draw attention to one place in Revelation where numbers—even numbers imbued with symbolic importance—simply are insufficient. The "great multitude" of Revelation 7:9 is a powerful reminder of God's inexhaustible compassion. In a book full of mysterious symbols, one thing is clear: God cares for us profoundly.

Lutheran Context

Two theological themes come to the forefront here. First is a question about worship. Worship can easily become rote, a habit we can fall into without much thought. Revelation's unique visions of heavenly worship—beautiful but also strange—can remind us of the true reasons we worship God.

 Political instability: Living under the Roman Empire was incredibly difficult. Every aspect of life was dictated by a distant ruler who could not be voted out of office. To make matters worse, this ruler was often seen as a living deity. Such power meant that the emperor and his officials could target a minority population, like ancient Christians, without any fear of recrimination.

 Economic limitations: One of the primary differences between the ancient world and today is economic. There was no middle class in the ancient world. Instead, there were minuscule numbers of wealthy elites; everyone else lived on very little. In a sense, the average person lived "paycheck to paycheck," with enough money for food for that day perhaps, but not enough to save for the future.

SESSION FOUR

Help lead participants into a reflection on the nature and purpose of worship. Why do we gather together on a weekly basis to sing and pray in worship? What kind of God is worthy of our worship? How are we as a people shaped by worshiping together?

The second theological theme is the question of the character of God. Many of us may tend to focus on the merciful character of God, and for good reason. God's mercy is a gift to us, and it is central to who God is. But God is also a just judge, an aspect of God's character that emerges regularly and powerfully in Revelation. In our culture, we strive not to judge others, so how is God's judgment different than ours?

Help participants think and talk about both aspects of God's character. In the end, Revelation teaches that God's mercy and God's judgment are interdependent; we cannot have one without the other. How do we hold mercy and justice together?

Devotional Context

The original audience of Revelation likely included people in need of hope in the midst of hopelessness. But they also yearned for that hope in the present day. That is, they would not have been satisfied with the mere assurance that everything would be fine one day. That kind of "hope" cannot deliver us from despair.

In the same way, therefore, we miss the mark when we try to comfort someone who has lost a loved one by pointing to the promise of heaven. That "hope" often does not bring comfort, because in such a time of loss we may be unable to look beyond our present pain. God too mourns our losses and does not seek to quench our pain with a promise of future deliverance. Instead, the visions of the future in Revelation are meant to address the present day. The vision of the 144,000 and the "great multitude" are meant to inspire us here and now by reminding us that God is faithful to God's promises, that God will always be victorious, that God ensures the deliverance of God's people.

Of course, this hope does not erase our troubles, and it is difficult to hold on to when life is falling apart. Help participants reflect together about how difficult it can be sometimes to keep hoping and to keep trusting in God. Together think about how these visions in Revelation help us think in new ways about God's care for us.

SESSION FOUR

Facilitator's Prayer

God of unfailing light,
in your realm of glory
the poor are blessed,
the hungry filled,
and every tear is wiped away.
Strengthened by this vision,
may we follow in the way of holiness,
that your Son is made known in life and death. Amen.
(*Revised Common Lectionary Prayers*, Augsburg Fortress, 2002)

Gather (10–15 minutes)

Check-in

Invite learners to share completed homework or any new thoughts or insights about the last session. Be ready to give a brief recap of that session if necessary.

Tip: As you near the midpoint of the course, check in with participants. Ask them to share when they felt most and least engaged in the Bible study. What can you learn from their responses and discussions? Starting this week, think about what adjustments you might make as a teacher and leader.

Pray

Join us now, God, as we open your Word. Fill us with wonder and curiosity, and guide us with your wisdom. In the midst of confusion, we ask for the clarity your Spirit brings. In the midst of despair, we ask for your comfort and calm. In the midst of hopelessness, show us the path of hope and expectation that Jesus himself walked. Amen.

Focus Activity

Study the woodcut that is the Focus Image for this session. What stands out to you? Where do you see hope in this depiction of Revelation?

Tip: Even more woodcuts dealing with Revelation are available at www.pitts.emory.edu/dia/woodcuts.htm.

Open Scripture (10–15 minutes)

Have participants form two or three small groups. Ask each small group to work together to present the text in a creative way to the large group. After these presentations, explore the similarities and differences between approaches.

Tip: The first option for hearing the text might also be a fine way to conclude this session. Informed by the Bible study, how do participants understand this text in new and creative ways?

As a volunteer reads the Bible text, encourage participants to use a pencil to underline any words or phrases that stand out to them or that they would like to know more about.

Session 4: Revelation 6:15—7:17

SESSION FOUR

Read Revelation 6:15—7:17.
- What emotions does this text evoke in you?
- What questions do you have about this text?
- Where do you see yourself in this text?

Join the Conversation (25-55 minutes)

Literary Context

1. At the beginning of Revelation 6, Jesus the Lamb opens the seven seals on the scroll. With each seal, visions of destruction emerge in the form of the "Four Horsemen," the cries of Christians who died for their faith, and finally a terrible earthquake. In Revelation 6:15-17 everyone in the world, from the powerful to the meek, flees these disasters in trepidation.

- Recollect some recent natural disasters that received media coverage. How did you feel watching these events? How might it have felt to live through such disasters? If you have experienced a natural disaster firsthand, what was that like?

Tip:
As you reflect on recent natural disasters, consider together how you might be of help to those in need. Collect money for donations or find other ways to help those affected.

Bonus Activity:
Print out or project news images of some recent natural disasters. Ask participants to reflect on their feelings as they see these images. Can they imagine themselves in these scenarios? What hope does Revelation offer in the midst of such tribulation?

2. For the first readers of Revelation, suffering and oppression were daily threats if not realities. These believers stood at the bottom of the world's power structure and had little recourse if the Roman Empire decided to exert its will against them. With the sealing of Israel's tribes and the diverse multitude in white robes, Revelation reminds readers that God promises to care for God's children. Even as the world seems to be falling apart all around us, God's promises will be fulfilled.

- Read Revelation 7:15-17. Discuss the promises given here, and how you see these promises being fulfilled in your own life today.

Bonus Activity:
Read Revelation 6:1-14. Provide art materials of various kinds. Have each participant depict the results of opening one of the six seals. (You may need to assign these so that all six seals are depicted.) What do you learn in seeing the depictions of the six seals?

Historical Context

1. From warfare to gladiatorial games and animal sacrifice, violence and the shedding of blood were more visible to ancient people than they are to most of us today. Though mass media regularly depicts violence and reports violent crime, there is a qualitative difference between the exposure to violence we experience and what ancient people experienced.

Bonus Activity:
Brainstorm together a list of God's characteristics or attributes. Write these ideas on a whiteboard or large piece of chart paper. Are there ways to group some characteristics together? Which attributes of God do we tend to highlight, and which do we tend to avoid?

- Some people see a distinction between the way God is portrayed in the Old Testament and the New Testament, arguing that the God of the Old Testament is violent and focused on punishment, while the God of the New Testament is peaceful and focused on grace. What do you think about this?

42   Revelation Leader Guide

- Read Revelation 6:15-17. How do violence and punishment play a role in God's work here? How might the original readers of Revelation have looked at this? Talk about how today's cultural context might make a difference in how we look at the violence and punishment in Revelation.

2. In the session text, numbers again play an important role in Revelation. In the midst of tribulation and mayhem, four angels hold back the winds while 144,000 receive the seal of God. These numbers represent the fullness of Israel, the chosen people to whom God keeps God's promises. Along with the tribes of Israel, people "from every nation, from all tribes and peoples and languages" (Revelation 7:9), stand before God in worship.

- Reread Revelation 7:9. In a book full of numbers, here there are more people than anyone could count! How important do you think it is that the writer doesn't include any kind of number here?
- What do you imagine eternity with God and God's people is like? Share some thoughts about this with a person sitting next to you.

Lutheran Context

1. Look beyond the dragons and four horsemen to see the importance of worshiping God in Revelation's visions. Acts of worship are a central component of Revelation's picture of heaven.

- Review Revelation 6:15—7:17 and discuss what this text tells us about worship. What is the point of worship, according to Revelation?
- Brainstorm a list of reasons why we worship. What effect does worship have on your life of faith?
- Sing or read together the words of "Behold the Host Arrayed in White" (ELW 425).

2. Just as Scripture includes both law and gospel, God's work in Revelation includes both judgment and mercy. God metes out judgment against the world (see Revelation 6:17) and saves the faithful from great tribulations.

- How do judgment and mercy affect your understanding of God? How do they affect your everyday life?

Bonus Activity:
Marcion was a second-century Christian leader who argued that the God of the Old Testament was not the same as the God of Jesus and the New Testament. He posited that the God of the Old Testament was cruel, vengeful, and violent, while the God of Jesus was gracious, merciful, and loving. Discuss why Christians have rejected Marcion's teachings.

Tip:
Consider using one or more of the worship ideas developed in the Bonus Activity as an introductory activity for next week's session.

Bonus Activity:
Have participants form groups of three or four, and ask each group to develop a short worship experience based on the session text. A group might create a brief drama, creative reading, or litany. Other options include finding hymns and songs that highlight the themes of the text.

Bonus Activity:
Give participants a few moments to think about a time they have felt God's mercy most sharply in their lives. Then ask them to think about a time they have felt God's judgment most sharply in their lives. Finally, ask them to discuss how these two experiences hold together. (Focus the discussion on the tension between God's mercy and judgment, and not on the details of the personal experiences.)

SESSION FOUR

 Bonus Activity:
Consider showing the thought-provoking video called "The Rapture," by Peter Rollins (vimeo.com/26809652?iframe=true&width=80%&height=80%). The video is a visual retelling of a parable by Rollins. How do participants feel about this video? How and what does this parable teach? How does it help us understand Revelation in a new light? (Be sure to prescreen the video to ensure that it is a good fit for your group.)

 Tip:
Encourage participants once again to journal, blog, or note insights into their reading of Revelation between sessions.

Devotional Context

1. Revelation's visions of heavenly deliverance can bring us comfort in the midst of distress, but they do not prevent us from dealing with the pain of loss, grief, and death in this life. This is especially true when we lose someone we love. We may find comfort in knowing that our loved one is welcomed into the arms of God in the afterlife. At the same time, we experience sadness and grief. We rage against the injustice of loss and the cruelty of death.

- Reflect on a time when you or someone you know faced loss, grief, or death. What was that experience like? Was the hope of a heavenly afterlife comforting in any way?

2. Pray and worship together using the words of Revelation. First, use Revelation 7:12 as your prayer. Move through the text slowly, reflecting deeply on each of the things God deserves. Pause after saying "blessing." Pause after saying "glory" and "wisdom," and so forth. Take time to dwell with these individual words. Then move to Revelation 7:15-17, using these verses as words of praise to God. To draw yourself closer to this scene, replace "they" with "we" and "them" with "us." At the close of your prayer and worship, reflect together on the experience.

Wrap-up

1. If there are any questions to explore further, write them on chart paper or a whiteboard. Ask for volunteers to do further research to share with the group at the next session.

2. Invite participants to share a word or phrase about Christian hope. Consider going around the room or circle to give everyone a chance to speak. (Also give participants the option to "pass" if they wish.)

3. Encourage members of the group to share any insights about God or God's mercy and judgment.

Pray

God of the ages,
your saints who lived in faithful service
surround your throne
and offer you praise and worship both night and day.
May we, your saints on earth,
join our voices with theirs to proclaim

*your rule of righteousness and peace,
which comes to us through Jesus Christ
now and forever. Amen.*
(*Revised Common Lectionary Prayers*, Augsburg Fortress, 2002)

Extending the Conversation (5 minutes)

Homework

1. Read the next session's Bible text: Revelation 12:1-17.

2. Like much of the rest of the book, chapters 6 and 7 in Revelation are full of powerful images, including the four horsemen, destruction at the opening of the seals, and the multitude of white-robed believers. Pick one or two images or scenes and do an online search for art depicting them. What themes do you see in this artwork? What similarities and differences do you see between these pieces? Next, turn to your artistic side. Pick a scene and create your own depiction. What themes do you want to emphasize? How is your faith reflected in your art?

3. Spend some time learning about the persecution of Christians and other people of faith around the world today. Begin by searching recent news reports and visiting the Web sites of The Voice of the Martyrs (www.persecution.com) and the Anti-Defamation League (www.adl.org). Think about what your Bible study group might do to support fellow believers, and what obligation we as Christians have to care for people of faith who are persecuted, no matter their beliefs.

Enrichment

1. If you wish to read through the entire book of Revelation during this unit, read chapters 12–17 this week.

2. View the movie *I Am Legend* (Warner Bros., 2007), which imagines a world that has fallen apart. New York City lies in ruins and is empty of human life except for one survivor. How could anyone survive as the last person left on earth? What would drive you to live in the midst of such hopelessness? Reflect on our culture, why we find a movie like this entertaining, and what effect this type of film might have on us.

Tip:
I Am Legend is entertaining and thought-provoking but also a bit scary and includes significant amounts of violence. You may wish to prescreen the movie before showing it to your group.

SESSION FOUR

For Further Reading

Can I Get a Witness? Reading Revelation through African American Culture, by Brian K. Blount. Louisville, KY: Westminster John Knox Press, 2005.

Enter the Bible (www.enterthebible.org).

Revelation and the End of All Things, by Craig R. Koester. Grand Rapids, MI: Eerdmans, 2001, pp. 81-92.

Looking Ahead

1. Read the next session's Bible text: Revelation 12:1-17.

2. Read through the Leader Guide for the next session and mark portions you wish to highlight for the group.

3. Make a checklist of any materials you'll need to do the Bonus Activities.

4. Pray for members of your group during the week.

SESSION FIVE

Revelation 12:1-17

Leader Session Guide

Focus Statement

The result of the great conflicts between God and the forces of evil is clear throughout Revelation. God, God's creation, and God's children are victorious.

Key Verses

A great portent appeared in heaven... Revelation 12:1a

And war broke out in heaven... Revelation 12:7a

Focus Image

Albrecht Dürer, *The Apocalyptic Woman*, © SuperStock/SuperStock

The Great "Battle"

Session Preparation

Before You Begin...

The seventh trumpet has just sounded as Revelation 11 closes, and the next chapter brings a dazzling but also frightening set of images. At the center of these images are judgment and promise: judgment against the forces of evil that seek to destroy God's chosen people and God's earth, but a promise to all who believe. The lamb that was slain (Revelation 4 and 5) remains victorious.

Session Instructions

1. Read this Session Guide completely and highlight or underline any portions you wish to emphasize with the group. Note any Bonus Activities you wish to do.

2. If you plan to do any special activities, check to see what materials you'll need, if any.

3. Have extra Bibles on hand in case a member of the group forgets to bring one.

Session Overview

In chapter 12 Revelation once again dazzles us with fantastic but often confusing images. As a dragon precipitates a war in heaven, a woman represents and embodies the deepest hopes of Christians everywhere. Behind these powerful symbols is a simple truth: despite all evidence to the contrary, God's care for God's people is inexhaustible and never-ending.

HISTORICAL CONTEXT

The primary thing contemporary readers might miss in the session text is the cultural and political resonance of the story that is told. The narrative of a pregnant woman imperiled by a pursuing dragon is not original to Revelation. Instead, here the writer draws on a well-known and often cited mythical story. The original version of this tale narrated the birth of Apollo. One of Apollo's first great deeds was the destruction of a massive serpent named Python. Revelation melds these stories together. Eventually, Roman emperors like Domitian claimed this birth story as their own, placing themselves in the role of the endangered child who, though pursued by his enemies, survived to rise and bring peace to the world and in the process became divine.

SESSION FIVE

For Revelation, this allusion is not just a way to tell an interesting story but a profoundly political assertion. The pretensions of Caesar and Apollo are ultimately unfounded. They are only pretenders on the world stage, for neither shares the throne with God.

So Revelation uses a well-known story in the culture, one that powerful emperors had already claimed as their own, to tell an entirely different story. The powerful of the world are only deluding themselves. The lamb that was slain, who is also the lion of Israel, is more powerful through weakness than mere mortals who use violence, fear, and trepidation as weapons to control the world. In contrast, God reaches out for us in love and compassion.

Literary Context

How do we make sense of the story that John tells? From a literary perspective, you and your group will approach this in two ways: through examining the symbols in the text, and through storyboarding the scenes.

Like the most powerful symbols in our culture, the symbols in the session text do not point to only one person, institution, or thing. Revelation itself provides the most important clues for interpreting its symbols and images. The task here is to trace how the images develop. In 12:5, for example, we learn that the woman gives birth to a child "who is to rule all the nations with a rod of iron." This is clearly Jesus Christ. Who then is the mother? She could represent Mary, the mother of Jesus, of course, but she could also represent Israel, the chosen people from whom and for whom the Messiah comes. Her image also shifts as the chapter closes and we learn that she is a mother to Jesus but also to all those who believe in Christ.

> **? Satan:**
> In ancient Jewish and Christian imaginations, Satan was an evil figure characterized primarily as a deceiver and an accuser. Satan seeks to trick the faithful into turning away from God, and when they do so, Satan is ready to bring their crimes before God in accusation. For more details, search for "Satan" at enterthebible.org.

Revelation 12 also draws our eyes to the great adversary **Satan**. Satan appears in the form of a dragon with seven heads and seven crowns. The seven heads may relate to the seven hills on which Rome is built, and the seven crowns are Satan's attempt to claim power over the world. Of course, this power does not belong to him. Satan's false claim to power is challenged by **Michael** and all the angels. They defeat Satan, but not entirely. Satan's wrath continues as he pursues the woman and her children. Even as the dragon roars, however, the earth itself fights back (12:16).

Even if some of the symbols remain unclear, the central conviction behind them is eminently clear. The dragon cannot be victorious, for God alone sits on a throne and only Christ is

SESSION FIVE

the lamb, who gains true power through weakness. In a sense, using the story of Apollo's birth undercuts the purported might of Rome and promises God's deliverance of the faithful who today are being harmed by the world. In short, God wins, and of that we can be certain.

As we study the literary context of a text, we can use tools from the field of writing and literature. Novelists, playwrights, screenwriters, filmmakers, and many others use storyboarding to create a visual outline of the scenes in a story. Some storyboards are works of art in themselves, but simple rough sketches or drawings are all that is needed to capture the characters, action, and setting involved in each scene. Creating a storyboard for Revelation 12 will engage you and your group with the text in a different way, and may draw out new insights as well.

Lutheran Context

Although the references aren't always direct, the writer of Revelation has a lot to say about Jesus. We continue to ask in this session, "What shows forth Christ?" This Lutheran principle for reading and interpreting the Bible encourages us to come to Scripture expecting Christ to come to us.

Paradox is another Lutheran insight on Scripture that comes into play again with this session text. Jesus is a lion and a lamb. God is a source of mercy and judgment. These images are not at odds for John, but wholly interdependent.

Devotional Context

For the earliest Christians, evil was a real and ever-present force in the world. That evil was personified in the figure of Satan, who is embodied in Revelation 12 as a massive seven-headed dragon. This dragon represents the present reality of evil, not just some cryptic image. Although he appears imposing and dangerous, ultimately the dragon is a powerless pretender. His defeat is assured.

The focus in our culture on the fantastic images, violent moments, and cryptic messages of Revelation tends to lead to misreading the text and overlooking the powerful statements of faith contained in the book: God is holy and sits on a throne, yet cares for us profoundly. God sides with us and will not desert the world. God will reign victorious, even as it looks like evil is prevailing. God is the true ruler of the earth. God is always with us.

 Michael:

In the ancient world, angels were messengers from God. In the Bible, they deliver messages to God's people. In Revelation, in particular, angels are the arm of God. They engage in a great heavenly battle in Revelation 12. Some angels in antiquity were known by name, including Michael, who here leads the armies of God against Satan's forces. Daniel 10:13, 21 and 12:1 also refer to Michael by name.

SESSION FIVE

Tip:
Apocalyptic movements are never too far from the view of the news media. If or when a new apocalyptic group is in the news, refer to it during a session. Help participants reflect on the motivations of the group and in what ways they do and do not line up with Revelation.

Tip:
Feel free to do an online search to find other depictions of Revelation 12. Comparing and contrasting the sixteenth-century woodcut and a more recent piece of art could highlight how differently this fantastic text can be pictured.

Tip:
"The Brick Testament" Web site offers a fun and provocative way to think anew about biblical texts. Because the Web site often depicts some of the more salacious and scandalous portions of the texts, be sure to preview how a text is depicted before using a rendition with Bible study groups.

Facilitator's Prayer

God of love, draw near to us as we read your Word. God of justice, show us the way of righteousness. God of compassion, lead us on the paths of righteousness. God of the beginning and the end, hold us in your care all our days. Amen.

Gather (10–15 minutes)

Check-in

Invite learners to share completed homework or any new thoughts or insights about the last session. Be ready to give a brief recap of that session if necessary.

Pray

God of all protection, grant us peace as we open your Word. Draw us together as we seek your wisdom and listen for your voice anew. In our fear, grant us peace. In our trembling, grant us hope. As we wait for your justice, help us remember your promise to never leave us or forsake us. Amen.

Focus Activity

The Focus Image is an artist's rendering of a scene in Revelation 12. What feelings does this artwork evoke in you? What stands out to you in the scene?

Open Scripture (10–15 minutes)

Pair the reading of this text with its rendition on the Web site "The Brick Testament," which tells biblical stories with the help of Legos and humor. Go to www.thebricktestament.com/revelation/satan_thrown_to_earth/rv11_15-18.html or locate it in the Revelation section under "Satan Thrown to Earth." Project the images, changing pictures as the text is read. After you finish the reading, ask how the images helped or hindered participants from understanding the text.

SESSION FIVE

OR

Encourage the group to doodle during the reading of the text, focusing on what captures their imaginations and not on drawing the scene.

Read Revelation 12:1-17.
- In what ways do you find this text troubling?
- What seems hopeful in this text?
- What do you find most confusing?

Join the Conversation (25–55 minutes)

Historical Context

1. The story of a dragon seeking to kill a pregnant woman would not have sounded strange to people in the ancient world. They would have been familiar with the story of Apollo being born in a similar threatening situation. In fact, this story was so well known and so powerful that Roman emperors placed themselves in it as Apollo! Used in this way, the story showed that although he was threatened by metaphorical dragons (that is, barbarians), the emperor survived and provided peace for his people.

- Why do you think Revelation 12 taps into a popular story of the time?
- How do Christians today continue to interact with popular culture?

2. Angelic figures played a prominent role in Judaism in Jesus' time. Angels were seen as messengers of God; they were intermediaries between the divine and humans. In Revelation, angels bear messages from God in the form of both words and actions.

- Reread Revelation 12:7-9. What is the "job description," or the role and function, of the angels here?

 Tip:
There is more to myths than false stories and Greek and Roman mythology. Myths help us order our experiences and make sense of a disorganized world. These larger-than-life stories tell us something about who we are. Help participants think broadly about the kind of myths (both positive and negative) we embrace every day in our culture.

 Bonus Activity:
Have individuals or small groups rewrite Revelation 12 as if it were written today. What great myths of our time might they tap into? How might they rewrite and retell a myth like *Star Wars*? How might they rewrite and retell historical myths?

 Bonus Activity:
Lead a discussion about a recent song, television show, or movie that has been particularly successful. How do we as Christians react to pop culture? What aspects of this song, show, or movie do we reject? What aspects do we find helpful to faith? Do Christians all deal with pop culture in the same way? Why or why not?

SESSION FIVE

Tip:
Prior to this session, look at the notes on Revelation 12 in a good study Bible such as *Lutheran Study Bible* (Augsburg Fortress, 2009) and *The HarperCollins Study Bible* (HarperOne, 2006). Your pastor or others in your congregation also might have suggestions on helpful commentaries and resources on Revelation.

Bonus Activity:
As an alternative to making a storyboard, have groups of two or three depict the scenes of Revelation 12 with a short poem or short story, a skit, or some other creative work. The basic idea here is to re-create the scenes in some other form to help everyone understand the text more deeply.

Bonus Activity:
Brainstorm on a large white board or piece of chart paper all the main characters and symbols in Revelation 12. The learner guide contains four that may be the most important, but there are several others. Then discuss to whom or what these main characters and symbols might point. Reflect together on why Revelation might opt for symbols in this instance. Why not simply say who the pregnant woman or the dragon represents?

Tip:
Create your own list of references to Jesus in Revelation 12 to help you start the conversation and perhaps highlight additional references to Jesus.

Literary Context

1. Let's unravel some of the symbols in Revelation 12. Who or what might each of the following characters represent? What Bible verses seem to support the connection you are making? (Feel free to use a study Bible. You'll find clues in chapter 12, the rest of Revelation, and other books in the Bible.)
- The pregnant woman
- The dragon
- The woman's son
- The wilderness

2. Even more important than unraveling the symbols is discerning what the session text teaches about who God is and how God cares for us. But with all the action in the story, unfamiliar images, and different characters, how can we grasp everything that is happening in Revelation 12:1-17? Storyboarding, a tool used by novelists, playwrights, screenwriters, filmmakers, and other storytellers, can help us by depicting the action, characters, and settings in a series of smaller, more manageable "scenes."

- As a group, create a storyboard showing the various parts of the story in Revelation 12:1-17. First, determine how many scenes you will need for the chapter. Second, draw or sketch each scene on a single piece of paper. Third, post the scenes in order around your meeting space.

- Take a step back and look at your entire storyboard. What portion was easiest to draw? What was most difficult to re-create? Make a list of themes and images that appear throughout the story. In one sentence, what would you say is the overarching story or message in Revelation 12?

Lutheran Context

1. As we learned in session 3, Lutherans expect all of Scripture to point to Christ. So "what shows forth Christ" in Revelation 12? There is a reference to the "Messiah" (12:10), but Jesus is not directly named until the end of the chapter (12:17). At the same time, Jesus is powerfully present here.

- List references to Jesus and his work as you reread Revelation 12:1-17. Note what each reference says about Jesus. Overall, how does Revelation 12 imagine Jesus and his work?

52 Revelation Leader Guide

2. Once again in Revelation, God's protection or mercy and God's judgment stand together. The images of the heavenly throne room (Revelation 4) and the lamb that was slain (Revelation 5) are meant to anchor our thoughts here and throughout Revelation. There will be a good ending for this book and for Christians all around the world, because God is in control and the lamb is victorious. Evil will be defeated, and the church will rest in God's protection.

- What words of judgment do you find in Revelation 12:1-17? What words of promise, protection, or mercy are given here?

Devotional Context

1. Despite popular images, Revelation does not exactly picture Satan as a horned figure with a long tail. Yet Satan does play a central role in the book. In ancient Jewish and Christian imaginations, Satan was a tempter and an accuser and "the deceiver of the whole world" (Revelation 12:9). Satan draws believers away from the path God has set before us and then brings our sins before God so that we stand accused.

- What do you think about Satan as a tempter and accuser? What do you understand Satan to be?

2. Revelation 12:1-17 promises that God will deliver us from all trouble and will never desert us. Think of a time when you felt all alone in this world. In what ways did you sense God's presence or protection with you at that time? (Or maybe you recognized God's protection later, as you looked back on what happened.)

Wrap-up

1. If there are any questions to explore further, write them on chart paper or a whiteboard. Ask for volunteers to do further research to share with the group at the next session.

2. In what ways does the text of Revelation 12 provide comfort in your life? In what ways does this text still confuse you?

Bonus Activity:

Have participants make lists of the promises of God they have noticed so far in Revelation, then share their lists with two or three other people. At the end of this discussion, have them trade their lists with someone else. Tell participants to take home their lists of God's promises and post them where they can be seen every day for the next week as a constant reminder of God's promises to them and their fellow believers.

Bonus Activity:

We are now more than halfway through the study, so take a moment to reflect together on what you have learned about Jesus, in particular, in Revelation. What new insights have you gained? What questions do you still have? Lead a large-group discussion on these questions.

Tip:

The themes in the Devotional Context this week might draw some participants to reflect on uncomfortable matters. Remind the group that the study is a safe space but that no one is required to share, especially when dealing with sensitive matters of faith and life.

Bonus Activity:

Spend some time in prayer for individuals in your community and in the wider world who are in need of God's hope and consolation. First, spend some time sharing about individuals and communities for whom the group will pray. Encourage participants to maintain confidentiality for individuals who may not want their names shared. How does Revelation teach us to pray for them and even for ourselves?

SESSION FIVE

 Tip:
Read aloud the first, third, and fifth lines of this prayer. Invite participants to join in on the second, fourth, and sixth lines (printed in bold).

Pray

God is our light and our salvation,
our refuge and our stronghold.
From the rising of the sun to its setting,
we praise your name, O God.
For with you is the fountain of life,
and in your light we see the light.
(ELW, p. 309)

Extending the Conversation (5 minutes)

Homework

1. Read the next session's Bible text: Revelation 18:1-24.

2. Go to the resources on the book of Revelation available at www.enterthebible.org and watch the video titled "Imagery." What do you think about Craig Koester's interpretation of Revelation's dazzling and often frightening images?

3. Rewrite Revelation 12 using images and ideas that would resonate with people today. Remember that John taps into a piece of popular myth used in the ancient world by emperors to help buttress their power. If John were to write today, what images would he use? Consider bringing your new version of Revelation 12 to the next session to share with others.

Enrichment

1. If you wish to read through the entire book of Revelation during this unit, read chapters 18–20 this week.

2. View the movie *The Road* (Dimension Films, 2009), based on the brief but powerful novel of the same name by Cormac McCarthy (Vintage, 2007). The book and film both recount the harrowing and hopeful journey of a man and his son striving for survival in a world turned completely upside down. Whether you watch the film or read the book (or perhaps even both!), consider what it might be like to live in a world where your very safety is constantly at risk. This was the experience of many early believers and continues to be the experience of many Christians today. Where do you see hope and promise in what is admittedly a very dark story?

SESSION FIVE

For Further Reading

Enter the Bible (www.enterthebible.org).

From Patmos to the Barrio: Subverting Imperial Myths, by David A. Sánchez. Minneapolis: Fortress Press, 2008.

"Revelation 13: Between the Colonial and the Postcolonial, a Reading from Brazil," by Vítor Westhelle, in *From Every People and Nation: The Book of Revelation,* ed. David Rhoads. Minneapolis: Fortress Press, 2005, pp. 183–199.

Looking Ahead

1. Read the next session's Bible text: Revelation 18:1-24.

2. Read through the Leader Guide for the next session and mark portions you wish to highlight for the group.

3. Make a checklist of any materials you'll need to do the Bonus Activities.

4. Pray for members of your group during the week.

SESSION SIX

Revelation 18:1-24

Leader Session Guide

Focus Statement
Revelation is an intensely political book. It undermines the preeminent political force of the ancient world by declaring that the power of the Roman Empire is nothing compared to the power of God.

Key Verses
"Fallen, fallen is Babylon the great!" Revelation 18:2a

"Alas, alas, the great city, Babylon, the mighty city! For in one hour your judgment has come." Revelation 18:10b

Focus Image

Gustav Doré, *The Fall of Babylon*, © iStockphoto.com / Ivan Burmistrov

The Fall of a Great and Powerful Empire

Session Preparation

Before You Begin . . .

Power is infectious. Power is assertive. Power can make us and break us. Power is at the center of Revelation 18. Here, the power of Babylon takes center stage. Yet for John Babylon is only a code name for Rome. For us, any empire, any massive exertion of power is our Babylon. How did God view these power centers then? How does God view these power centers today?

Session Instructions

1. Read this Session Guide completely and highlight or underline any portions you wish to emphasize with the group. Note any Bonus Activities you wish to do.

2. If you plan to do any special activities, check to see what materials you'll need, if any.

3. Have extra Bibles on hand in case a member of the group forgets to bring one.

Session Overview

Revelation is written from the perspective of the powerless. As John writes from exile on Patmos, suffering under a political system of oppression, he imagines a world where God's justice is the order of the day. How do we understand empire today? How do we claim God's justice in a still-unjust world?

HISTORICAL CONTEXT

In the coded language of Revelation 18, we are reminded of a stark reality for the author of Revelation and its first readers. Challenging Rome was a potentially deadly activity. In an **empire** like Rome, dissent was not considered an expression of free speech. Rome viewed any opposition as treason. Therefore, when John wishes to point out the many injustices perpetrated by the Roman Empire, he must do so with great care so his readers don't find themselves accused of looking for the overthrow of the state.

This is precisely why in Revelation 18 the writer speaks of "**Babylon**" when referring to the Roman Empire in which the early Christians lived. Remember that John is in exile on the island of Patmos because of his beliefs (see Revelation 1:9). He likely wants his readers to understand that God will ultimately reign victorious, without exposing them to more danger from the state. By speaking of Babylon, John can point out the judgment of God over Rome without putting his readers at risk.

Rome's injustice runs deep, and the evils of the empire don't trace back only to the emperor. Instead, a whole set of economic and political structures support Rome's power and ensure its existence. Enriched by the power of Rome, merchants and shipmasters alike side with Rome because of all the benefits the state can provide. Meanwhile, little thought is given to those crushed along the way.

Literary Context

Revelation asserts boldly that empires will eventually fall under their own weight, that the accumulation of wealth and cruelty that sustains Rome will eventually be its downfall. As Rome tramples over more and more people, the empire cannot stand. As the wealthiest and most powerful live in luxury while the rest of the world suffers, the empire withers. As evil grows, empires fall.

But notice that Babylon doesn't fall in Revelation because the people overthrow the reigning power. Instead, God's justice guarantees the toppling of evil. God is continually working to bring God's justice to an unjust world.

Revelation 18 pulls us in two directions. It invites us to look forward and anticipate a day when God's justice reigns. But it also demands that we look within our own lives and examine whether we also are entangled in oppressive systems.

This text poses a particularly difficult challenge for modern Christians in the West. Biblical scholar Michael J. Gorman states it this way: "It would be easy to assume that most careers and day-to-day practices are exempt from critique, but Revelation will not allow us to be so naive. If it involves buying or selling goods, Revelation subjects it to question. Is this a business that directly or indirectly promotes the rich and exploits the poor? Does it harm the earth or other human beings? If so, then Revelation 18 addresses it" (*Reading Revelation Responsibly: Uncivil Worship and Witness; Following the Lamb into the New Creation* [Eugene, OR: Cascade Books, 2011], p. 149).

Empire:
Empire is a political structure wherein a small number of people hold nearly unilateral power over a wide swath of land and peoples. The writer of Revelation maintains that the accumulation of power and wealth among a select few eventually leads to an empire's downfall. In the meantime, the rest of the people face suffering, injustice, and cruelty.

Babylon:
Babylon was a powerful city in modern-day Iraq, and at the center of a powerful empire of the same name in the second and first millennia B.C.E. In 597 B.C.E. the Babylonians deported Israelites from Jerusalem. This period of exile is the background for many portions of the book of Isaiah.

SESSION SIX

Lutheran Context

As we have learned throughout this study, Revelation is not an easy book to read and interpret for today. For a number of reasons, this book stretches our faith in often uncomfortable and challenging ways. The Lutheran tradition has a way to help clarify such difficult passages of Scripture. Instead of reading these texts in isolation, Lutherans often turn to other texts of Scripture to help bring light and insight into these complicated words.

Let's do just that with Revelation 18. Here, looking at a number of texts from the Gospels will help participants reflect on the intertwining of love and justice found in Revelation 18. How is it that a God of love also demands justice? Should we celebrate when an evil empire crumbles?

The aim in these exercises is to help broaden our imaginations around God's sense of justice as expressed in all these passages. The Gospel of Luke is riddled with dramatic reversals: the powerful will be stripped of their thrones, the hungry will be fed, the broken will be made whole.

God accompanies those among us who suffer. God walks alongside the oppressed. God stands on the side of those crushed by the world. God will right the wrongs the world commits. God's justice is not about revenge. It is about creating a world in which all can live, thrive, and be in relationship with God.

Devotional Context

When the world seems most unfair, the word of God can be a valuable resource for us. The Bible can remind us that God will never desert us. It can assure us of God's love for us and the promises God has made. Scripture can also give us a path through which we can express our frustrations with injustice in the world. It can provide us with hope but also give shape to a cry of disappointment and dejection. It can show us God's way of righteousness but also allow us to rage against a world where God's will is not the order of the day.

Rage, anger, and frustration are feelings that are often difficult for us to express in our faith. We don't often make room for such feelings. Revelation provides us an ideal opportunity to learn some biblical language around these concerns.

SESSION SIX

As you complete the exercises or Bonus Activities, make time to reflect on the propriety of these feelings in our faith. Do participants agree that there is space for rage and frustration in our faith? How do we express these feelings in accordance with God's grace for us?

Facilitator's Prayer

Give ear to my words, O LORD; give heed to my sighing.
Listen to the sound of my cry, my King and my God, for to you I pray.
O LORD, in the morning you hear my voice; in the morning I plead my case to you, and watch. (Psalm 5:1-3)

Gather (10-15 minutes)

Check-in

Invite learners to share completed homework or any new thoughts or insights about the last session. Be ready to give a brief recap of that session if necessary.

Tip:
Make space for participants to pose questions or share insights they have gathered over the last week. As they pondered the texts, did new ideas emerge? As they lived everyday life, did something in Revelation come into their minds at unexpected moments?

Pray

God of mercy, lead us to embrace your love for us. God of justice, lead us to walk in the paths of your righteousness. God of never-ending love, hold us as we open your Word. Grant us open ears, hearts, and minds to be changed and renewed for your sake. Amen.

Tip:
Pray by reading in unison or go around the room with one person taking one sentence of the prayer. Invite participants to extend the prayer with their own supplications.

Focus Activity

The Focus Image depicts the fall of Babylon, a mighty city in the ancient Babylonian Empire. As you look at this image, imagine for a moment the tumult and distress that would come with the fall of a great city. As some mourn, why might others rejoice?

Tip:
In a number of movies, the destruction of iconic cities is part of the powerful visuals. Think for example of the end of *Planet of the Apes* (Twentieth Century Fox, 1968) when Charlton Heston discovers the remains of the Statue of Liberty, or the frozen New York City in *The Day after Tomorrow* (Twentieth Century Fox, 2004). Consider juxtaposing an image from one of these films with the Focus Image.

Open Scripture (10-15 minutes)

Bring in an audio version of the NRSV Bible. Play the recording of the text as learners read along in their own Bibles.

Do an online search for images of recognizable and great cities of today. Post printouts around the meeting space and invite everyone to walk through the "gallery" as you read the text.

Tip:
There are a number of excellent audio versions of the Bible; some are free but many are worth the cost. Preview a few online before selecting one to use in this session.

SESSION SIX

Read Revelation 18:1-24.
- What surprises you in this text?
- What image seems most powerful to you?
- In one sentence, summarize what this text is about.

Join the Conversation (25–55 minutes)

Historical Context

1. Rome was ruling the world at the time he wrote Revelation, so why would John describe the demise of ancient Babylon? Why would the earliest readers of Revelation be interested in an empire that had fallen long ago? John's readers would immediately have associated these verses with a great and powerful empire, but generally not with Babylon. Revelation provides clues that make it clear we are dealing with Rome, not Babylon, here (for example, Revelation 17 points to the reigns of various Roman emperors; see a study Bible for more details).

- Brainstorm a list of reasons John might have chosen not to refer to the ruling Roman Empire directly.

2. Revelation 18 details the many people and industries willing to trample over "human lives" and slaves as part of Rome's cruel exertion of power. They were willing to buy into Rome's ideology of power and spread its corruption abroad as well. Though it appears invincible, John believes the Roman Empire is already poised for destruction, because its obsession with wealth and influence has led to unjust and cruel practices.

- Review Revelation 18. Make a chart with two columns to list responses to the fall of Rome (Babylon). In the first column, list the responses of the people and industries that are part of Rome's system of power and cruelty. In the second column, summarize John's response.

Literary Context

1. One of the main points in Revelation 18 is the corruption and evil of Babylon. The writer goes into great detail to support this point.

- Reread Revelation 18 and make a list of all of Babylon's crimes. In what ways did Babylon's corruption infect the whole world?

 Tip:
Use a whiteboard or chart paper to record participants' responses.

 Bonus Activity:
Rewrite Revelation 18 as if it were written today. What persons and industries might lament today as Babylon falls? Where do you see elements of "Babylon" in our world today?

 Bonus Activity:
As a group, create an artistic depiction of Revelation 18. Working together on one large piece of paper, draw or sketch the many images and symbols of this chapter.

 Tip:
Help participants to see that Revelation 18 pulls us in two directions. It looks forward to a day when God's justice reigns. It also demands that we ask ourselves difficult questions about whether we are entangled in oppressive systems.

- Reflect on how these sinful entanglements are present in the world today. What might we do about sinful systems like these, in light of Revelation 18? How are we affected by or involved in sinful systems?

2. The celebration of an empire's demise is not an unfamiliar scene or turn of events in history or in literature and films. Revelation boldly asserts that empires will eventually fall under their own weight. As the wealthiest and most powerful live in luxury while the rest of the world suffers, empires cannot stand.

- Name some powerful leaders, rulers, empires, and nations—from history or fiction—that were eventually overthrown. What kind of power did they have or claim to have? What led to their fall? How did people react when they were overthrown?
- What kind of power do you see used by leaders, rulers, "empires," or nations today? What might the writer of Revelation say to them and to us?

Lutheran Context

1. Using Scripture to interpret Scripture is a central practice of Lutheran interpretation, as mentioned in session 2.

- Read Luke 1:46-55. The Magnificat, the glorious song in this text, is sung by Mary, who will become the mother of Jesus. Here a very young, powerless woman cries for the deliverance that God will provide through her son. What similarities and differences do you find between this song and Revelation 18? How does Mary's song shed light on your reading of Revelation 18?

2. Let's use Scripture to interpret Scripture again. Turn to the Sermon on the Plain in Luke 6:20-26 (this is Luke's version of Jesus' Sermon on the Mount). What themes appear as you read Luke 6:20-26 and Revelation 18 together? How does the Sermon on the Plain shed light on your reading of Revelation 18?

 Bonus Activity:
Reflect together on the role Christians should play in political matters. Some participants may have strong feelings and opinions on this topic. Ask the group to set aside partisan matters for the moment. Talk together about how Revelation 18 inspires or reshapes how you think about the involvement of Christians with the state.

 Bonus Activity:
Have participants talk with one or two others about the ethics of their daily activities. Whether you are a full-time parent, a mechanic, a business executive, or retired, think about how your faith influences what you do. Is there a time in which your ethics and your faith have been put to the test?

 Tip:
Print out the biblical texts you will be studying so that participants can spread them out on a table and read all of them together without flipping pages over and over. Encourage the group to use underlining, circles, and so on to note similarities and differences between these texts.

 Bonus Activity:
Add Zechariah's song (Luke 1:67-79), called the Benedictus, to the comparison. What similarities and differences do you find between this song and Mary's song? In what ways does each song resonate with Revelation 18?

 Bonus Activity:
Add the Sermon on the Mount in Matthew 5 to the comparison. What do the sermons in Luke and Matthew share? In what ways are they different? In what ways does each resonate in special ways with Revelation 18?

SESSION SIX

Tip:
People in your group may have varying degrees of comfort with finding frustration, anger, and bitterness expressed in Scripture. Consider discussing what the expression of these feelings says about the relationship between God and the writers.

Tip:
Have copies of ELW available, and make arrangements for any musical accompaniment in advance.

Bonus Activity:
As you read the text of Revelation 18, invite participants to create two lists of emotions they sense as they hear the text read again. In one list, have them note what emotions Revelation 18 relies on or appeals to in those who read or hear it. In another list, have participants note what emotions they sense in themselves as they hear the text read. On chart paper or a whiteboard, record responses for both lists. What significant overlaps between the two lists are present? What significant differences do you see? Reflect together on the meaning of these commonalities and distinctions.

Tip:
Remind participants to keep track of new questions and insights they gather throughout the week. At the beginning of next week's session, invite them to share these questions and insights.

Tip:
Before using this prayer, remind participants of the meaning of the marriage imagery found here. Who is the groom? Who is the bride?

Devotional Context

1. The rage of an oppressed people reaches a full roar in Revelation 18. All the anger and frustration that have built up in John and his community find voice as the text rejoices over the fall of a great but destructive empire.

- Read Psalm 137. In this text, exiles from Jerusalem lament to God and rage against the injustice of being forcibly taken from their homes (notice especially the violent words of verse 9). How are Revelation 18 and Psalm 137 similar?
- Talk about whether there is room in our faith today to express frustration, anger, and bitterness.

2. Revelation 18 shows God's response to great cruelty and injustice. Tell about a time you experienced a great injustice, witnessed a great injustice in the life of a friend or family member, or heard about a great injustice in a newscast. How did this injustice affect you and your faith? List some ways you could respond to this situation.

3. Sing together "God of Grace and God of Glory" (ELW 705).

Wrap-up

1. If there are any questions to explore further, write them on chart paper or a whiteboard. Ask for volunteers to do further research to share with the group at the next session.

2. What has inspired you in the study of Revelation 18? What has challenged you?

3. Are there specific ways the study of Revelation has shaped your faith in the last six weeks of study? Invite participants to share some of their experiences.

Pray

"Hallelujah!
For the Lord our God the Almighty reigns.
Let us rejoice and exult and give him the glory,
for the marriage of the Lamb has come,
and his bride has made herself ready;
to her it has been granted to be clothed
with fine linen, bright and pure." (Revelation 19:6b-8a)

SESSION SIX

Extending the Conversation (5 minutes)

Homework

1. Read the next session's Bible text: Revelation 21:1-8.

2. Read and study Revelation 17 with the help of a study Bible and any other resources available from your church or elsewhere. What do you think about the images in this chapter? How do you apply this text to your life?

3. Do an online search for news articles on modern-day slavery and other oppressive economic systems. How might Revelation 18 speak to these injustices? What might your Bible study group do to bring awareness of these exploitive practices to your church and community?

Enrichment

1. If you wish to read through the entire book of Revelation during this unit, read chapter 21 this week.

2. *The Book of Eli* (Alcon Entertainment, 2010) stars Denzel Washington as a lone traveler in a post-apocalyptic world. His mission is to protect a sacred book that holds the keys to a new world. After watching the film, reflect on how the movie resonates with themes found in Revelation 18. How can Revelation help us examine our daily practices and involvement in political and economic systems that may be harming others?

For Further Reading

From Patmos to the Barrio: Subverting Imperial Myths, by David A. Sánchez. Minneapolis: Fortress Press, 2005.

Reading Revelation Responsibly: Uncivil Worship and Witness; Following the Lamb into the New Creation, by Michael J. Gorman. Eugene, OR: Cascade Books, 2011. (See especially pp. 145-159.)

Looking Ahead

1. Read the next session's Bible text: Revelation 21:1-8.

2. Read through the Leader Guide for the next session and mark portions you wish to highlight for the group.

3. Make a checklist of any materials you'll need to do the Bonus Activities.

4. Pray for members of your group during the week.

Tip:
Lutheran World Relief (www.lwr.org) provides excellent resources for learning about and helping in matters of injustice today. Think about supporting the work of this organization as you contemplate the message of Revelation.

SESSION SEVEN

Revelation 21:1-8

Leader Session Guide

Focus Statement
Revelation promises that our current and future homes are strikingly similar and yet qualitatively different. The renewed creation brings to full fruition God's original hopes for the world.

Key Verse
Then I saw a new heaven and a new earth; for the first heaven and the first earth had passed away, and the sea was no more. Revelation 21:1

Focus Image

NASA Goddard Space Flight Center Image by Reto Stöckli (land surface, shallow water, clouds). Enhancements by Robert Simmon (ocean color, compositing, 3D globes, animation). Data and technical support: MODIS Land Group; MODIS Science Data Support Team; MODIS Atmosphere Group; MODIS Ocean Group. Additional data: USGS EROS Data Center (topography); USGS Terrestrial Remote Sensing Flagstaff Field Center (Antarctica); Defense Meteorological Satellite Program (city lights). Image courtesy of NASA.

Our New Home Is Here but Not Here

Session Preparation

Before You Begin . . .

Too often, when Christians reflect on heaven, we find ourselves transported into the clouds, into a place that has no resemblance to life on earth. However, the vision of a new heaven and a new earth in Revelation 21 leads us to consider God's work of creating the earth anew today and in the future.

Session Instructions

1. Read this Session Guide completely and highlight or underline any portions you wish to emphasize with the group. Note any Bonus Activities you wish to do.

2. If you plan to do any special activities, check to see what materials you'll need, if any.

3. Have extra Bibles on hand in case a member of the group forgets to bring one.

Session Overview

Revelation 21 provides a tantalizing glimpse into our eternal homes. It also represents the fulfillment of every promise God has made to the world. The depiction of these future realities is about the present as much as it is about the future. It is supposed to give us not only a vision of the future, but an impetus and imagination about what life today might look like for the faithful.

HISTORICAL CONTEXT

In the end, our eternal homes are right here on earth. Revelation 21 narrates how God calls down a **new Jerusalem** in the process of creating "a new heaven and a new earth." Peace and serenity are the order of this new day. Distress and anxiety are vestiges of a long-forgotten past.

The "first heaven and the first earth" (that is, the world as we know it today) pass away and the sea is no more (21:1). If you are someone who loves going to the beach, this is rather distressing! Remember, however, that the sea for many ancient Jews was a symbol of chaos and danger, a place where boats would be tossed and easily dashed against the rocks with capricious changes in the weather. Here, Revelation is not imagining a placid afternoon in a beach chair but the roiling waters of a merciless sea. In the end, this new heaven and new earth leave behind the chaos, plagues, and destruction that marked the preceding chapters of Revelation.

This would have been profoundly good news for a people facing persecution and oppression from the Roman Empire. The supposed **Pax Romana** was but an illusion. For the earliest Christians, hope rested not on the powers that governed them but on the God who promised eternal safety.

LITERARY CONTEXT

The closing chapters of Revelation are conclusions to three different "books." They bring the book of Revelation, the New Testament, and the whole of the Christian Bible to an end. And what an ending this is!

The work God starts in Genesis comes to a beautiful culmination. What happens in Revelation 21 is not a repeat of the flood. It does not involve wiping the slate clean and starting again. Instead, the whole world is created anew. The heavens and the earth are transformed into God's original hopes for the world.

Once again, Revelation is about God more than it is about us. Revelation holds fast to a God who is consistent in keeping God's promises. Even as the world seems to fall apart in the middle chapters of Revelation, God remains in God's throne room (remember Revelation 4), which means that God continues to care for us as much as ever.

In Revelation 21, God's care for us is spelled out in beautiful ways. For example, Revelation 21:3 confesses that "the home of God is among mortals." That is, God walks with us in our lives. The power of God's presence is described in 21:22-23, where we learn that there is no temple in the New Jerusalem, because God's presence permeates every bit of that city. God is palpable throughout this new city. The sun and moon are also unnecessary, for God's glory provides its powerful light to the city.

This is our new home.

 New Jerusalem:
Revelation 21:9-27 provides several details about this incredible new city. Its construction is deeply symbolic. The number twelve, for instance, is a symbol of God's promises to Israel. The city is a cube representing its powerful structure and perfection, and it is made of precious jewels and metals. In addition to all of this, the city is massive; in modern measurements, each side of this city is fifteen hundred miles long!

 Pax Romana:
The Roman Empire promoted the notion that its power ensured the peace of the whole world. The claim was that with peace came a stable economy and safety for the public. This peace, however, came at a great price. Violence and oppression were often deployed by the empire to ensure the continuation of "peace."

SESSION SEVEN

Lutheran Context

Revelation's theological vision is bold and ambitious. As readers of Revelation, we are called to be no less bold and ambitious.

In these verses, John recalls the very first days of God's creation of the world. The new heavens and the new earth are a return to this experience of paradise, but with important changes. God is powerfully present in the midst of creation, but instead of a garden populated with two individuals, John imagines a massive city teeming with people from all over the world. In this new creation, God commits to life with us. The new Jerusalem is not aloft in the heavens but firmly planted on God's good earth.

Finally, the new Jerusalem is a city with gates that never shut for fear of foreign invasion. Indeed, those kings of the earth who had previously created a false peace based on violence and fear now find themselves drawn into this glorious city.

Remind participants that this vision of an incredible future is meant to help us, here and now, understand who God is and how we ought to relate to our neighbor.

Devotional Context

Revelation's vision for the future is not intended to dull our senses and distract us from the pains we experience every day. Rather, the vision of a new heaven and a new earth is meant to inspire us to think differently about our current situation. If this heavenly city is our future home, how should we live right now? If God will live in our midst, how do we relate to God right now?

If you do an online search for images of "heaven," it is likely that all you will get are gauzy images of places that look nothing like earth. These visions of heaven are radically different from the new heaven and new earth in Revelation.

Our eternal home awaits us. But it is also true that our home is right here! God intends to complete the work God started in Genesis 1. That work comes to culmination on the earth God created, not in some ethereal space in the clouds. Notice, for example, the promise that "mourning and crying and pain will be no more" (Revelation 21:4). What might it look like for Christians to collaborate with God in helping craft a world in which the conditions that cause mourning and crying and pain

SESSION SEVEN

are brought to an end? For Christians to collaborate with God in drawing near to those who mourn, cry, and are in pain? For us to be the hands and feet of Christ to these people?

Facilitator's Prayer

Sovereign of the universe, your first covenant of mercy was with every living creature. When your beloved Son came among us, the waters of the river welcomed him, the heavens opened to greet his arrival, the animals of the wilderness drew near as his companions. With all the world's people, may we who are washed into new life through baptism seek the way of your new creation, the way of justice and care, mercy and peace; through Jesus Christ, our Savior and Lord. Amen. (From ELW, p. 81)

Gather (10-15 minutes)

Check-in

Invite learners to share completed homework or any new thoughts or insights about the last session. Be ready to give a brief recap of that session if necessary.

Pray

Alpha and Omega, First and Last,
glory outshining all the lights of heaven:
pour out upon us your Spirit
of faithful love and abundant compassion,
so that we may rejoice in the splendor of your works
while we wait in expectation
for the new heaven and the new earth you promise
when Christ shall come again. Amen.
(*Revised Common Lectionary Prayers*, Augsburg Fortress, 2002)

Focus Activity

Think for a moment about the most beautiful place you have seen on earth. Now think about distressing places you've seen. As you look at the Focus Image, talk about how the world can be so beautiful but also so ugly at times.

Tip:
Invite prayer requests and pay special attention to anyone who expresses concern about a loved one who is nearing death. The discussion of eternal life and heaven in this session could provoke both comfort and anxiety for them, so be aware of how they are interacting during the session.

Tip:
Plan ahead and bring pictures of some of the most beautiful places you have seen on earth. Encourage others to do the same in the days leading up to this session.

Session 7: Revelation 21:1-8   67

SESSION SEVEN

Tip:
This session focuses on Revelation 21:1-8, but the rest of the chapter is quite important in understanding John's vision of a new heaven and new earth. Spend some time prior to the session reading and studying the entire chapter.

Tip:
Alpha and Omega are the first and last letters of the Greek alphabet, so "I am the Alpha and the Omega" is another way of saying, "I am the beginning and the end." In English, God might say, "I am everything, from A to Z."

Bonus Activity:
Provide a number of art supplies and invite participants either to depict the new heaven and new earth of Revelation or to imagine their own version of a new heaven and a new earth. Invite individuals to share their work with someone else and talk about what was easiest to capture in a picture and what was most difficult.

Bonus Activity:
Bring in a brief article describing what you think is the most important news of the week. Discuss together how John might have reacted to this "breaking news" if he were writing Revelation today.

Open Scripture (10–15 minutes)

As a volunteer reads the biblical text, encourage participants to underline any words or phrases that stand out to them or that they would like to know more about.

Read the text aloud outdoors or at least move near a large window in your church or to some other space where participants can see outdoors while you read the text. Before you begin reading, ask listeners to imagine what a new heaven and new earth might look like in your community.

Read Revelation 21:1-8.
- What do you imagine "a new heaven and a new earth" would look like?
- What feelings arise as you listen to this text?
- What word, phrase, or image stands out to you?

Join the Conversation (25–55 minutes)

Historical Context

1. As we near the end of Revelation, God's victory has been won definitively—though that was never in doubt. Evil is defeated, and the work God began at the dawning of creation now comes to its final fruition. And, John writes, the sea is no more. This may sound strange to us, but for many ancient Jews the sea was a symbol of chaos and danger, a place where boats could be tossed and easily dashed against the rocks with capricious changes in the weather. In the end, this new heaven and new earth leave behind the roiling waters of a merciless sea—the chaos, plagues, and destruction that marked the preceding chapters of Revelation.

- Revelation 21:1 says the "first heaven and the first earth [that is, the world as we know it today] had passed away, and the sea was no more." How might this have been good news for a people facing persecution and oppression under the Roman Empire?
- What might be a symbol of chaos and danger for us today, and what images might we use for the peace and serenity of the new heaven and new earth?

2. It is no accident that the new Jerusalem in Revelation 21:2 is a beautiful city: "This 'paradise' is not just a garden but an urban

68   Revelation Leader Guide

garden or, even better, a *garden-city*. This tells us that it is not civilization/culture/the city itself that is evil, but the distortion of city/culture/civilization caused by evil people and powers" (Michael J. Gorman, *Reading Revelation Responsibly: Uncivil Worship and Witness; Following the Lamb into the New Creation* [Eugene, OR: Cascade Books, 2011], p. 164). Rather than starting over with a blank slate, God meets us where we are. God cleanses our cultures, our cities, and our civilizations from all evil. That is, God loves the world God created. God loves our cultures and civilization. What God cannot abide is how human cruelty and injustice have corrupted these wonderful things God created.

- What aspects of our culture today need God's cleansing? What aspects of the world need to be made new?

Literary Context

1. Notice that the first words of Revelation 21 speak of a new heaven *and* a new earth together. Often, when we think about the end, we imagine only heaven—a place beyond the earth, not on it. But Revelation promises both a new heaven and a new earth.

- How does the re-creation of both heaven *and* earth reflect who God is and what God is like?

2. Revelation's story is set within the larger story of the New Testament, and the even larger overarching story of the Bible. Read Genesis 8:20-22 and note the promise made by God to Noah and his family. How is the transformation of the world in Revelation 21 connected to this? What does this tell us about God?

3. Perhaps the most striking portion of Revelation 21 is found in the lyrical words of verses 3 and 4. God will dwell with us. God will comfort us in all our despair. God will defeat Death once and for all.

- Reread Revelation 21:3-4 aloud together. How might these promises influence your life today? How might this vision of heaven shape your faith?

Lutheran Context

1. In many ways, the vision of Revelation is audacious. It looks to encapsulate and imagine all of human history culminating in one fantastic vision of God's new creation. Again using the principle of Scripture interprets Scripture, we reach all the way back to the opening chapters of Genesis to shed light on these closing chapters of Revelation.

Tip:
Invite a conversation about our faith and ecology. What significance does our hope in a new heaven and a new earth have for our efforts today to preserve God's creation?

Bonus Activity:
Have participants form small groups of twos or threes to read through Revelation 21 and make lists of everything that is excluded from the New Jerusalem. Then ask groups to make lists of what is found in the New Jerusalem. Taking a step back, have participants discuss how the two lists make them feel about God's hopes for our lives together.

Bonus Activity:
Have participants form small groups of twos or threes to respond to the following questions: Whom do you expect to see in heaven? Why? Would it be difficult or disappointing for you to find certain individuals there? Why or why not? How does Revelation address these hopes and concerns?

Tip:
Consider making copies of any texts you plan to use in the activities. That way, participants can read all of the texts side by side.

SESSION SEVEN

 Bonus Activity:

Compare Revelation 21 to Isaiah 65:17 and 66:22. What might it mean that God was already promising a new heaven and a new earth in the book of Isaiah? How do these verses in Isaiah help you better understand Revelation?

 Bonus Activity:

Is heaven a future reality alone, or is there some way we can have a taste of the new heaven and the new earth? Invite participants to think about a time in their lives when they felt close to heaven. That is, when did they feel most at peace, most at home, and/or happiest? Have them share responses with one other person, noticing what their experiences have in common. In what ways does Revelation reflect these experiences?

 Tip:

Have copies of ELW available. Consider having an assortment of simple percussion instruments on hand for the song as well.

 Bonus Activity:

As difficult as it may be to do, have participants think about their own funerals. Would they want Revelation 21 to be read at the service? Why or why not? How much would they want the promise of heaven and eternal life with God to figure into this service?

 Tip:

Ask participants to reflect this week on what they have learned about Revelation and what questions they still have. Encourage them to record these insights and questions in some way and bring them to the next session.

- Read Genesis 1. How do Genesis 1 and Revelation 21 together speak about God and God's creation?

2. Law and gospel, mercy and judgment are at work in Revelation 21. Read Revelation 21:24-27 and list who is invited to walk into the gates of the New Jerusalem. What does this teach us about God? How do you see both law and gospel active in this text?

Devotional Context

1. Think about your own life or the life of a child or grandchild. What kind of life would you hope for? What would be an ideal life? Discuss how your hopes for the future shape your words and actions right now.

2. Our culture tends to imagine heaven with certain stock images: pearly gates, clouds floating in the sky, angels flitting around. In what ways do visions of heaven shape your faith? Create a piece of art (for example, a drawing, painting, poem, dance, song) that shows how you imagine the new heaven and new earth of Revelation 21.

3. Sing "Soon and Very Soon" (ELW 439).

Wrap-up

1. If there are any questions to explore further, write them on chart paper or a whiteboard. Ask for volunteers to do further research to share with the group at the next session.

2. When you think about the future, what inspires hope? What inspires fear?

SESSION SEVEN

Pray

*"See, the home of God is among mortals.
He will dwell with them;
they will be his peoples,
and God himself will be with them;
he will wipe every tear from their eyes.
Death will be no more;
mourning and crying and pain will be no more,
for the first things have passed away."* (Revelation 21:3-4)

Tip: As a group, pray this prayer aloud.

Extending the Conversation (5 minutes)

Homework

1. Read the next session's Bible text: Revelation 22:8-21.

2. Read about the New Jerusalem in Revelation 21:9-27. Using a study Bible and resources such as enterthebible.org, study the symbolism involved in John's depiction of this new city. What are its characteristics? How large is it? Why is its shape significant? What does it mean that God is the temple in this new city and provides all its light? Also do an online search of images of the New Jerusalem. How do these depictions of the city compare to the marvelous description in Revelation?

3. Using a smartphone or a small notebook you can always carry with you, take note this week of all the glimpses of "a new heaven and a new earth" you see in everyday life. In what ways, small and great, does God provide you with a foretaste of God's eternal glory in your everyday life?

Enrichment

1. If you wish to read through the entire book of Revelation during this unit, read chapter 22 this week.

2. Watch the movie *Up* (Disney/Pixar, 2009). Make this a multi-generational event by inviting others from your church to attend the screening. After the film, ask about the values of the movie and its characters. What is really important in life? What does "heaven" look like in this film?

Tip: The movie *Up* is fundamentally about hope in the future. What plans do we make and never fulfill? What hopes have we had dashed in our lives due to unexpected tragedy? What eventually drives us to chase our dreams with reckless abandon?

SESSION SEVEN

For Further Reading

"Revelation," by Brian K. Blount, in *True to Our Native Land: An African American New Testament Commentary,* ed. Brian K. Blount, Cain Hope Felder, Clarice J. Martin, and Emerson B. Powery. Minneapolis: Fortress Press, 2007.

"Revelation," by Susan R. Garrett, in *Women's Bible Commentary: Expanded Edition,* ed. Carol A. Newsom and Sharon H. Ringe. Louisville, KY: Westminster John Knox Press, 1998.

Looking Ahead

1. Read the next session's Bible text: Revelation 22:8-21.

2. Read through the Leader Guide for the next session and mark portions you wish to highlight for the group.

3. Make a checklist of any materials you'll need to do the Bonus Activities.

4. Pray for members of your group during the week.

SESSION EIGHT

Revelation 22:8-21

Leader Session Guide

Focus Statement
Living in the end of days should not inspire dread and trepidation in the heart of the believer. Instead, the promise that Jesus will return soon should propel us to act in hope, anticipation, and expectation.

Key Verse
And he said to me, "Do not seal up the words of the prophecy of this book, for the time is near." Revelation 22:10

Focus Image

Knocking at the Door, by He Qi, www.heqigallery.com

Jesus Is Coming Soon

Session Preparation

Before You Begin . . .

As fearsome as some of the images of Revelation are, the final word of this powerful book is not trepidation but hope. The promise that God loves us and holds us is a word of hope in a world full of much tragedy.

Session Instructions

1. Read this Session Guide completely and highlight or underline any portions you wish to emphasize with the group. Note any Bonus Activities you wish to do.

2. If you plan to do any special activities, check to see what materials you'll need, if any.

3. Have extra Bibles on hand in case a member of the group forgets to bring one.

Session Overview

Why do we read Revelation? Many Christians avoid Revelation because they are afraid of and confused by it. In this last session of the study, help participants reflect on how they have come to understand this difficult book in new ways. Every question won't be answered, and every difficulty won't be solved during this study. The aim is to become active interpreters of Revelation in our daily lives.

HISTORICAL CONTEXT

As we look back on our study of Revelation, let's remember how Revelation begins, with letters to seven churches. This is not an insignificant detail. Instead, it shows us several things:

- Revelation is not just abstract reflection but a word of encouragement or warning to a number of real communities. John thought of specific communities and their specific challenges and concerns as he wrote.

- This book was decipherable to its first audiences. They could understand what John was writing. Certainly, some of Revelation's symbols may have been difficult to understand, but the book was written to address their pressing concerns. All in all, John is not an **esoteric** writer but a pastoral theologian.

SESSION EIGHT

> **? Esoteric:**
> An esoteric piece of literature assumes only a few select people will fully understand the writing. Such writing is not meant to be read widely. While the writer of Revelation uses symbols—like equating Rome and Babylon—in order to criticize the empire subtly, these symbols are meant to protect John and his readers from the charge of treason, not to hide his real intentions. John expects that all his Christian readers will be able to understand this writing.

- This book is about the present as much as it is about the future. Again, Revelation addresses real communities with real concerns. In imagining a future characterized by God's deliverance and God's justice, John hopes to shape how these churches live at the present time.

- Thus, this book is about faith and hope, not fear or anxiety. Whether a church found itself under the burden of oppression or was guilty of being too comfortable, the good news of Revelation is that God's reign knows no end.

- Despite the specificity of the book's original audience, John seems to assume that others will read his vision as well. Thus, we are properly recipients of this good news along with John's first readers.

Literary Context

The final verses of Revelation include a number of small summaries, short sentences meant to remind us of where we've been but also of what John hopes his readers will take with them.

Therefore, this is a good time to remember that the central vision of the book is found in Revelation 4-5. The closing chapters of the book confirm the truth of that vision. Despite all evidence to the contrary, God rules and rules alone. Jesus is made powerful through weakness. As the book closes, much has changed, and the whole world has been transformed. Some things, however, have not changed whatsoever. God's character and Jesus' faithfulness persevere.

Also, we must remember that the long shadow of Roman power should shape how we understand Revelation. To put it simply, the Roman Empire was the most significant reality John and the seven churches faced. Its economic, political, and military might meant that the empire and its powerful reach were part of their daily lives.

To imagine at that time that there was any power beyond the Roman Empire was bold, requiring a huge leap of faith. It is precisely this faith in God that brings us to the end of this book. It is precisely faith in Jesus' return that draws these Christians into a promised future. Now, it is our turn. Can we trust in God and God's promises? Can we look forward to Jesus' return in hope and expectation, not with trepidation? In short, can we have faith today?

SESSION EIGHT

LUTHERAN CONTEXT

For too long, many Christians have ceded theological ground to fanciful eschatological dreamers who treat the living word of God as a mere puzzle to be solved, a **complex cypher** only the purportedly enlightened can decode. But Revelation challenges us to return to that sense of expectation that imbued the faith of Jesus and his earliest followers with so much power.

Revelation is not a salve or opiate for the masses. Revelation does not provide an excuse to sit on our hands as we await the end. Instead, this text can help us think about what is ultimately important. It can help sharpen our vision, fill out our hopes, and express our deepest fears. These reflections on the end are really about the present day. These reflections teach us not how we will live in the future as much as how to live now.

Ultimately, Revelation is not about providing a road map to the end of days. Revelation narrates a radical way to shape how we relate to God and one another today. Revelation invites us to a posture of trust in God and God's work. Revelation is not really about bold predictions of days yet to come. Revelation is instead about seeing the work of God in big events but also in the seemingly ordinary, even unremarkable, moments of each day.

DEVOTIONAL CONTEXT

Revelation is different, isn't it? It is not like the Gospels, chock-full of stories of Jesus healing and teaching. We can easily picture ourselves in these powerful scenes. Revelation is not like the letters of Paul, packed to the brim with passionate reflections on the meaning of Christian community. We can usually hear ourselves addressed in these ancient letters. We have to work just a bit harder to hear Revelation speaking to us directly. But the effort is well worth it.

Remember that theological reflections about the end were a central part of the faith of the earliest Christians. When we read Revelation, we join our sisters and brothers across the span of time. When we avoid Revelation, we miss this precious opportunity.

So, in this final session, encourage participants to turn to Revelation with boldness, hope, and expectation. Remind them that fear, confusion, and apprehension are not the characteristics of God's work in Revelation or in our lives.

 Complex cypher: Too often, Christians have tended to read Revelation as if it were a magical Bible code—if we could just figure out the meaning of its symbols, we would have a precise road map to the end of days. This is not what Revelation is all about. It is not a puzzle or riddle that only really smart or really spiritual people can figure out. It is a book for all Christians, which the Holy Spirit can help us all read together.

SESSION EIGHT

We look to Jesus' return with hope. We hope for a new world where justice and righteousness overcome hate and division. We hope for the death of death. We hope for life everlasting. We hope for the easing of our many griefs. We hope for the kind of joy only God can provide. In the end, this is good news! Don't be afraid. Jesus is coming soon.

Facilitator's Prayer

"Holy, holy, holy,
the Lord God the Almighty,
who was and is and is to come."
"You are worthy, our Lord and God,
to receive glory and honor and power,
for you created all things,
and by your will they existed and were created."
"To the one seated on the throne and to the Lamb
be blessing and honor and glory and might
forever and ever!"
Amen. (Revelation 4:8b, 11; 5:13b)

Gather (10–15 minutes)

Check-in

 Tip: Since this is the last session of the study, prepare to provide a bit of extra time for the check-in. Participants may want to voice the "big questions" they have been grappling with over the last seven sessions.

Invite learners to share completed homework or any new thoughts or insights about the last session. Be ready to give a brief recap of that session if necessary.

Pray

Creator of the universe,
you made the world in beauty,
and restore all things in glory
through the victory of Jesus Christ.
We pray that, whenever your image is still disfigured
by poverty, sickness, selfishness, war, and greed,
the new creation in Jesus Christ may appear in justice,
love, and peace,
to the glory of your name. Amen.
(Revised Common Lectionary Prayers, Augsburg Fortress, 2002)

76 Revelation Leader Guide

SESSION EIGHT

Focus Activity

On an index card, write three things you have learned about God, Jesus, and faith during this study of Revelation.

 Tip:
Let the group know you will be posting the index cards. When everyone is done writing, collect the cards and post them around your meeting space. Give participants time to walk around and read what others have written. Then discuss points of overlap. Also, invite participants to take one of the cards and place it in their Bibles at the beginning of Revelation, as a reminder of the work you did together in this Bible study.

Open Scripture (10–15 minutes)

In pairs or trios, take turns reading the text to each other and listening carefully as the text is read.

 OR

Ask listeners to gravitate toward a single word or phrase from the reading that they will later share with the group, along with reasons why that word or phrase stood out to them.

Read Revelation 22:8-21.

- Do you think this is a good ending for the book of Revelation? Why or why not?
- What messages do you find repeated over and over again in this text?
- What questions come to mind as you hear this text?

Join the Conversation (25–55 minutes)

Historical Context

1. "The time is near." "I am coming soon." The writer of Revelation assumes that the consummation of all things is right around the corner. He calls his readers to live in eager expectation and hope. Even as it looks like Rome's power is growing without end, there is only one true God we can trust: the God of Israel, the God of Jesus Christ.

- Nearly two thousand years later, what do the words "the time is near" mean for us? What does it mean for us to believe that Jesus is coming soon? Talk about how these promises are still powerfully true for us today.

2. Some of the last verses in Revelation are warnings to those who would read, interpret, and preserve this book for future generations. Remember what was said in session 1 about genre. Revelation is an apocalypse, meaning it is a work that purports to reveal information previously unknown and unknowable. The information is true because it comes from God, often through

 Tip:
Although you and your group have been reading "over the shoulders" of the first readers of Revelation, God continues to speak through Scripture today. You might ask participants what they think about this. What is God calling them to do or to be, through the words of Revelation?

 Bonus Activity:
Prior to the session, gather news articles or images that will help jog people's memories about the events of the last year. (Check year-end retrospectives in major newspapers and magazines.) As participants look back over the last year's events, discuss: What was the most tragic event in the news in the last year? If John were writing Revelation today, how might he address that tragedy? How do we translate Revelation's words of hope in the midst of distress to speak to new situations?

SESSION EIGHT

 Bonus Activity:
Show a YouTube video for a Chevy Silverado ad from 2012's Super Bowl XLVI. The video is at www.youtube.com/watch?v=XxFYYP8040A. In the commercial, only some trucks survive the 2012 Mayan apocalypse. What cultural values are assumed in this video? In what ways does Revelation lead us to think differently about the end than this commercial?

 Bonus Activity:
Ask participants what image or scene in Revelation has stuck with them most throughout this Bible study. That is, what image or scene keeps coming back to them, has troubled them most, or has given them the most hope? Using whatever art supplies are available, invite participants to create visual representations of these scenes or images. Then have them share this art with a partner and explain why they chose the image they did.

 Bonus Activity:
Suppose for the moment that you meet a Christian who has never read Revelation. In groups of two or three, have participants create a "top-ten list" of the most important things to know before and as you are reading Revelation. In other words, what has been most helpful to you and your group members as you have read Revelation in this Bible study? Ask participants to share their top-ten lists with other members and leaders of the congregation who were not able to participate in this study. Encourage others to read Revelation and your pastor to preach on the book.

 Tip:
For question 3, go around the group and invite each person to respond (or to "pass" if they wish). If your group is large, have participants form groups of two or three to share responses.

an intermediary like an angel. This is surely part of John's motivation in warning his readers to keep this text exactly as it stands. These words have come from God to us. They should not be changed. John also seems to assume that others beyond his own immediate community will read and copy his words. (Why warn readers not to change his words if John did not expect them to copy and share this powerful text?)

- In what ways have we been reading "over the shoulders," so to speak, of Revelation's first audience? In what ways is Revelation nonetheless God's word for us today?

Literary Context

1. After writing twenty-one chapters of letters and visions—both beautiful and horrifying—John turns to speak to his readers directly as he ends Revelation with a collection of summaries and closing thoughts. These are not as well integrated and do not flow as smoothly as other parts of the book, but there is much richness here. It is almost as if John is feverishly rushing to remind us of just a few more things.

- Reread Revelation 22:8-21 and list the main topics and ideas John communicates here.

2. The "tree of life" that stands in the midst of God's garden in Revelation 22 is an image from Genesis 2 and 3.

- Read the following texts: Genesis 2:9; 3:22-24; and Revelation 2:7; 22:1-5, 14. What is the significance of the tree of life in Revelation 22, the final chapter of the Bible? What promises of God does it signify?

3. Though many think of Revelation as some sort of timeline for the last days, we have seen that this book is about God and Christ. All of Revelation rests on chapters 4 and 5, where we are first introduced to God on a throne and the lamb that was slain. These two images are at the very center of the book's convictions. What have you learned about God, Jesus Christ, and the Spirit in this Bible study? What new questions about God, Jesus Christ, and the Spirit have emerged for you?

Lutheran Context

1. Once again, Revelation pairs condemnation of evil with an open invitation for all people to come into God's healing presence.
- Review Revelation 22:8-21 and discuss how God's good news arrives as both law and gospel.
- How can Christians both condemn evil in this world and invite all people into the church?

2. Many people look at Revelation as a puzzle that ordinary people are incapable of solving, or a road map to the last days that only experts can decode. The Lutheran view, however, is that the meaning of Scripture is not a secret God shares only with certain individuals. Through public interpretation—as we read and study the Bible together—God speaks to us in powerful ways today.
- If a close friend or family member asked you what Revelation is all about, what would you say?
- Name one thing you have learned from reading and studying Revelation with the others in your group.

Devotional Context

1. Look at the Focus Image and reflect on how Revelation has shaped your faith over the last few weeks. In what way is Jesus knocking at your door? What has Jesus taught you in this Bible study?

2. Revelation closes with John's response to Jesus' repeated promise that he will return soon. John says simply, "Amen. Come, Lord Jesus!"
- Spend some time praying: "Amen. Come, Lord Jesus!"
- What would it mean in your life if Jesus were to come right now? What would change in your life? How would you prepare for Jesus' arrival?
- Look through the "End Time" section of ELW (hymns 433-441) and choose a hymn or song to sing together at the end of this session.

 Tip:
Ask participants to think back to the first session of this study. How often had Revelation been a part of their faith or their life in church? What has changed?

 Bonus Activity:
Post four large sheets of chart paper around the room. Write the following topics on the top of one of those pieces of paper: God, Jesus, Future, Faith Today. Provide time for participants to write a few words or a sentence about some new ways they understand each topic in light of Revelation. Then invite participants to walk around and read what others have learned.

 Bonus Activity:
On a whiteboard or large sheet of chart paper, have participants write three words that best summarize the messages of Revelation for them. Then step back and notice which words appear most often. Why are these the most common words?

 Tip:
Have copies of ELW available, and arrange for musical accompaniment if you wish.

 Bonus Activity:
People who live in areas where natural disasters like earthquakes or hurricanes frequently strike often have preparedness packages on hand, just in case. Discuss: What would you need to be prepared for any eventuality in your faith? What "supplies" would you pack in your spiritual preparedness kit? What are the most indispensable components and resources of your faith? What is most important in the end?

SESSION EIGHT

Tip:
Invite participants to contribute their own wrap-up questions. What are the big questions they take away from this study? What big questions are they still pondering?

Tip:
Another option for this closing prayer is to invite participants to pick their favorite prayers and words of worship from Revelation. Invite them to share these words from their Bibles as they feel so led.

Wrap-up

1. What have you learned about Revelation that you want other members of your congregation or a family member to know?

2. What in Revelation inspires you with hope?

Pray

God of boundless grace,
you call us to drink freely of the well of life
and to share the love of your holy being.
May the glory of your love,
made known in the victory of Jesus Christ, our Savior,
transform our lives and the world he lived and died to save.
We ask this in his name and for his sake. Amen.
(*Revised Common Lectionary Prayers,* Augsburg Fortress, 2002)

Extending the Conversation (5 minutes)

Homework

1. Reread Revelation again in one sitting. What new things do you notice in this reading that you didn't catch during the Bible study? What new questions do you have? In what ways does Revelation continue to speak to your faith in new ways?

2. Spend some time reading about apocalyptic movements in North America. There are many, such as the Millerites, Seventh Day Adventists, Branch Davidians, the groups led by Harold Camping, and the Mayan calendar hysteria in 2012. How might this reading influence how you read Revelation?

3. Pick a scene from Revelation that has lingered in your mind and spirit. Use your artistic abilities to capture your fascination with that scene, whether you are a poet, musician, painter, sculptor, or cook. Share your art with your friends and family.

Enrichment

1. Are there themes that emerged in the study that you would like to explore via film? Brainstorm a list of movies you might view as a group. Collect suggestions and come to an agreement on one film. As you view and discuss the film, celebrate the learning that you have done together.

2. Learn about the 10,000 Year Clock project that Jeff Bezos, the founder of Amazon.com, has funded. You can find information

about it at www.10000yearclock.net. In what ways does the project's vision of the future fit with that of Revelation? How do these visions differ?

For Further Reading

The Rapture Exposed: The Message of Hope in the Book of Revelation, by Barbara Rossing. New York: Basic Books, 2004.

Revelation and the End of All Things, by Craig R. Koester. Grand Rapids, MI: Eerdmans, 2001.

Revelations: Visions, Prophecy, and Politics in the Book of Revelation, by Elaine Pagels. New York: Viking Penguin, 2012.

Tip:
Consider following up this Bible study with a book study using one of the three books listed for further reading. These three books are all quite different, so spend some time previewing them online before choosing one.

www.ingramcontent.com/pod-product-compliance
Lightning Source LLC
Chambersburg PA
CBHW051421070526
44584CB00023B/3526